Advance Praise for
Old California Strikes Back

Old California Strikes Back is that rare thing: a truly original work. An inventive blend of history, hilarity, and outlandish fabrication, Scott Russell Duncan interrogates our collective dreams about California and wakes us up to its complex realities.

—Cristina Garcia

A unique voice, telling a unique version of California—a mix of fantasy, history with a post-modern look at Zorro, Helen Hunt Jackson's *Ramona*, and Joaquín Murrieta. Laced with sharp insights, bold critiques and acerbic humor, this book is crazy fun. Should be required reading for every Californio.

—Alejandro Murguía,
San Francisco Poet Laureate Emeritus

With *Old California Strikes Back,* wondrous wordsmith whiz, Scott Russell Duncan singlehandedly shocks back to life contemporary American letters. In his alchemical admixture of the fictional with the factual, he delivers a delicious picaresque metafiction that spins readers through a kaleidoscopic zany journey of a fictionalized Scott Russell Duncan, the true heir to a 19th century fictional character Ramona (created by the *real* Helen Hunt Jackson), in pursuit of an Anglo huckster who fancies himself a modern-day Zorro. With this, Duncan joins our pantheon of Latinx metafictional greats: Oscar "Zeta" Acosta, Fernando Flores, Carmen María Machado, and Salvador Plascencia.

He breathes life into his heirs apparent: Cortázar, Borges, Pynchon, Barth, and Barthelme. This is the Latinx novel we've all been waiting for. This is our *literature of replenishment* at its best!"

—**Frederick Luis Aldama**, award-winning author
and the Jacob & Frances Sanger Mossiker Chair
in the Humanities at UT Austin

Old California Strikes Back is a brash and surreal journey, with Scott Russell Duncan and his partner, the head of Joaquin Murrieta, galloping forward, not with guns blazing, but with two 19th century novels at the ready, *Ramona* and *The Life and Adventures of Joaquín Murieta*. Duncan kicks up a lot of dust with his novel, unsettling any notion about a fixed and figured out Chicano identity, and pissing off the heroes who were probably just villains all along. Reach for the book carefully, and then read with abandon.

—**Matthew David Goodwin**, Assistant Professor,
Department of Chicana/o Studies,
University of New Mexico

Old California Strikes Back

The Fantastic Return of a Californio

FLOWERSONG
PRESS

by

Scott Russell Duncan

FLOWERSONG
PRESS

FlowerSong Press

ISBN: 978-1-953447-01-2
Library of Congress Control Number (LCCN): 9781953447012

Published by FlowerSong Press
in the United States of America.
www.flowersongpress.com

Author Photo by Scott Russell Duncan
Image by Scott Russell Duncan
Cover Design by Alex Garcia, @elindioarts
Set in Adobe Garamond Pro

Dedication

Dedicated to my sister Laura who lived her own way and left us as she slept, as she dreamed.

Acknowledgements

This book was so long an albatross, finally slated to be published, it could be called a different bird, an owl, like the unwelcome portent Helen Hunt Jackson wore on her hat and terrified Native people, and like the giant one, big as a flying monkey, that terrified me as I saw it in the car's headlights before my sister's passing by her house. The manuscript of this novel went into the fire of my sister's Native funeral. We were born on this coast where so many of our Native mothers birthed us and were robbed of their ways until finally my sister had a ceremony which survived the two colonizations that so changed our family.

I started writing this book as a youngish man ready to have answers, a SRD/Joaquin Living Head/Zorro amalgam, dead sick of the questions that the lack of history and the colliding fragments of myself caused. The spinning top of Native, Mexican, White and being too much and not enough of any. I wanted and tried to write something new.

I dreaded my family reading it and now that they, my immediate family are gone, the rest is for me to tell and others to call me liar or leap and believe me, of all people.

This novel was the story of my family, my outsiderness, my belonging and my history, my Native being and my Chicanismo. It's a story of decolonizing and cessation of crossroads and fragments. Writing this did work. It healed. It hurt. If you love it or not. I'm changed beyond the ending, certainly from the beginning when I first wrote this. I'm in a Native space, a more resistive space than the conclusions, and reject the many settler labels thrown at me, Latinx, Hispanic, or Mestizo. When the novel started, I, a short story writer thought, how long would it take to finish this? Crap, two years? Probably.

Instead, writing the novel caused a heavy depression. I became less functional. I wanted a funny story about writing the book, something a little off, but one that would make it seem as if it was worth it. Rather, creating this book cost friends and my health, mental and physical.

I thought it would open doors for me to me, heal what has been called the permanent confrontation between the Native and the European. I tried. There is a cost seeking healing, ending the schizophrenic scar of colonization and I paid for the attempt. No regrets. Just wish it finished ages sooner.

I have many to thank, foremost my wife, Sonia. She's British, not British; an adventurous and plucky scientist, she put up with the madness of the book being written.

Dr. Carlota Caulfield had her work and research as an example and encouragement and knowledge of history and literature to help many times. Her experience and mentorship was invaluable.

Jenny Irizary somehow was always more confident in what I was doing than I and I will always thank her as well as the rest of my old writing group, Blanca Torres, Lisa Gray, and Juan Alvarado, all golden for different kinds of critiques and honesty and storytelling. Their work was always an inspiration to see develop and know it's possible to overcome through writing.

Thanks to Rosa Martha Villarreal for her insight and magic page number.

Thanks to every magazine editor who published an excerpt of this book through the years and helped keep me going.

Thanks to FlowerSong and poet and editor Edward Vidaurre for publishing this work and the work he and FlowerSong do for our community. Thanks to the dynamo representing raza, Califas, and SoCal throughout the world, poet Matt Sedillo, for bringing my work forward.

If you have ever asked for a blurb, you know how it makes you feel like a filthy urchin asking to spend a night in the master bedroom. I got amazing blurbs from amazing writers and scholars I hope my work deserves. Thank you to the collection of wonderful writers and editors who not only replied, who read the book and said better niceties than I could imagine: the great novelist Cristina Garcia, the editor and scholar Matthew David Goodwin, the scholar, writer and artist Frederick Luis Aldama AKA "Dr. Latinx", the fellow Californio and renowned poet Alejandro Murguía (who I need to thank again for writing *The Medicine of Memory: A Mexica Clan in California*).

@elindioarts AKA Alex Garcia is the artist best suited for the book. He had a better vision than I, the-down-to-the-truth, rather than the punk Native inverse of the Spanish fantasy lie. He gave the front cover what my book meant: the taking back of our tales, our heroes, our fragments. Our beheaded, yet still alive Chicano culture in the form of a vibrant defiant Joaquin. Thanks, Alex.

Speaking of cats, as always, this book wouldn't have been possible without plum pudding, kitty, sweet kitty, Jessie the cat who blinked or sneered as I read many of its passages out loud to my least receptive and most captive audience. She will be missed. And to my departed junkyard cat Ollie, whose joie de vivre and aggressive spirit didn't put up with any bullshit in what I was reading. And of course, to Pickles, the huntress and badass protector. Because of her I thought all cats would warn me of everything.

He didn't get in much, but thanks to my departed Uncle Billy Bob for taking me in when no one else did and helping me realize as a teenager that I am Brown as fuck and that this man who took me in is so White, he is ethnic.

Thanks to my whole family. Write your own book if you don't like it. The way out is through the supermarket. I love you guys.

I want to thank whoever reads this as well. Putting yourself on the page.

Last thing about this novel: there's more. Come and ask me to read and I'll read vignettes of the travel that did not make it into the slapped-together book Zorro received.

This book changed me. I hope it gives you pause and a chance to see potentialities for transformations and even more, to follow your own decolonial path.

Viva California! Viva la raza!

—Scott Russell Duncan

table of contents

"With the very fertile lands that the United States will be taking from us, with climates milder than any which they have possessed up until now, with brilliant port facilities for maritime commerce such as are offered by that inestimable jewel, Upper California, the US will cause Europe to empty out, gentlemen, and the European immigrants will amalgamate with the present population of the US and will take the lead in establishing themselves over us. Our race then, our poor people will have to become nomadic, searching for hospitality in foreign lands, only to be ejected later to still other places. As almost all of us are descended from Indians, the North American people abominate us, their orators depreciating us even while recognizing the justice of our cause. Since they consider us unworthy of forming with them a single nation or society, they have manifested clearly that in their future conquests they will strip us of our land and thrust us aside. Has their conduct, in fact, been any other in their treatment of the Indian tribes, former owners of the land which now belongs to those same United States?"

—Manuel Crescencio Rejón

"The way to kill a man or a nation is to cut off his dreams, the way the whites are taking care of the Indians: killing their dreams, their magic, their familiar spirits."

—William S. Burroughs

"A victim to the wickedness of a few men whose false pretenses were favored because of their origin and recent domination over the country, a foreigner in my native land, could I stoically be expected to endure their outrages and insults?"

—Juan Nepomuceno Seguín

"In great torment is my heart: as if it were washed in chili water
it indeed burns."

—Motecuhzoma Xocoyotzin

"*Los Chicanos,* how patient we seem, how very patient. There is the quiet of the Indian about us. We know how to survive. When other races have given up their tongue, we've kept ours. We know what it is to live under the hammer blow of the dominant *norteamericano* culture. But more than we count the blows, we count the days, the weeks, the years, the centuries, the eons until the white laws and commerce and customs will rot in the deserts they've created, lie bleached. *Humildes* yet proud, *quietos* yet wild, *nosotros los mexicanos*-Chicanos will walk by the crumbling ashes as we go about our business. Stubborn, persevering, impenetrable as stone, yet possessing a malleability that renders us unbreakable, we the *mestizas* and *mestizos,* will remain."

—Gloria Anzaldúa

"...en el Corazon del Corazon, el camino real stops here!"

—Alejandro Murguìa, *16th and Valencia*

Old California Strikes Back

The Fantastic Return of a Californio

1.
Zorro's Note

Before this book, I called myself Zorro. While my recollections differ, and I object to my depiction, the author of this tale, Scott Russell Duncan (SRD), and I do know each other—he has assaulted me on occasion, robbed me of personal property, pieces of clothing even (hats, capes, masks, scabbards), before disappearing and then reappearing only to deprive me once again. I can say SRD gives the impression of the deranged, the desperate, and, most of all, the zealous. And he had taken to traveling in a patchwork of styles derived from period clothing and artifacts lifted from various museums and private collections. Not the least of his artifacts is the human head which he has used to terrorize me numerous times.

Yet, at heart, we are kindred spirits: never have I met anyone whose passion for Californios so outmatched my own, and indeed, I found inspiration in his journey as I followed SRD, hoping to learn what he learned of Old California and of Ramona. Again, while the events in these pages differ and seem even more grotesque and fantastic than I remember, Mr. Duncan is correct in saying California is the place to find one's dreams. Hence, I will not correct him. Our last meeting did end in a brawl as I tried to reason with him until he stuffed me in a storage room on Rancho Moreno for a second time, which was when the latest "big one" hit. After I shoved beams and fallen bricks off myself and tried the doorknob and found it unlocked, he and his assorted band of the deranged and desperate were gone—along with all the inheritance of the Californios. What could I do but go home, go back East? Back to perpetual overcast and calm and away from the sunny palm trees and raging Pacific. There, after several weeks where I grew lonely and misanthropic reflecting on my life in California, this manuscript, a stained and stinking binding of divers papers that once had been a copy of my own book, scribbled over, tripped me up on my doorstep.

I will speak briefly on this Ramona Diary in the condition as it arrived at my door. (Ramona Diary? Read on, you'll find out). The origins of the stains and stenches that decorated and radiated from the manuscript were detailed and apologized many times by SRD to my wincing unhappiness as I read through the nest of papers. Not only does the diary suffer from disorganization, the numbering of diary entries drops off and leaves only achronological titles. Furthermore, he wrote upon pages torn from my own guidebook to Ramona's California, *True Son of Ramonaland*, as well as paper scraps, and the blank spaces of street flyers for rock bands and real-estate brochures. (And what seemed to be butcher paper, which I found most unpleasant as it contained the reek of the previously mentioned whiskey-pickled human head). SRD declares none of the stains were his doing, but he does list them as not-his-own-urine, not-his-own-excrement, not-his-greasy-food, not-his-hot sauce, and a chilling reference to not-his-own-blood, some of which must be mine as this manuscript was used during his many assaults upon my person, specifically, my nose. Adding to the compounded confusion, many entries, numbered or otherwise which are referenced, seemed to be lost—torn out by SRD or slipped out as he slinked across California, robbing its secrets. He also references several "book-plosions" and attempted willy-nilly re-bindings, utilizing his self-described legendary sewing skills. The cover, if one could call it, had been duct taped to the front and in what seems marked with black felt pen a series of crossed out potential titles, descending from the top:

~~Ramonaland~~

~~The Ramona Diary of SRD~~

~~Diary of a Quasi-vato~~

~~The Griffin Kitten Republic~~

~~Night of the Living Californios~~

~~El Camino Real Stops Here~~

~~My Heart is Bathed in Taco Sauce~~

~~Two-Heads of California~~

~~Wrestling Ramona~~

Ending in the middle, writ large:

OLD CALIFORNIA STRIKES BACK

The Fantastic Return of a Californio

This all, of course, creates a unique reading effect. An effect dear to those with interest in the Californio Mexican experience, I might have once called Spanish California, the American West, and moreover, the American imagination, and dare I say Native America. I have recreated this effect as best I could for the reader sans stains and with a more conventional uniformity of transcription and presentation, such as matching my guide's description of a Ramona site with the corresponding SRD diary entry, or the portions of my book underneath if pertinent. I have also limited my editorial voice to only this note to prevent any accusations of self-promotion and to diminish the confusion as the pages torn from my *True Son of Ramonaland* already contain my own vociferous statements.

What remains the proper or preferred order and method of reading such a text other than my attempt to present it as it was written down, I make no judgment to anyone wishing to dive into textual chaos and would offer alternate orders of readings if arriving at my own had not taken so much effort and a steel stomach. You are welcome, in other words, to read straight as Zorro can figure, or willy-nilly as befits the world we live in where beginnings and endings are arbitrary.

Reading and editing this manuscript has opened my eyes, however much SRD and Ramona complained of my dearth of character. They must have found me somewhat redeemable, despite my "dorky and prurient lust for the Californios," as it is to me whom they entrusted with the story of their return, *Old California Strikes Back*. Which I now offer up to you.

—**Zorro** (for the last time).

2.

True Son of Ramonaland: Starting Out!

Ramona! Who? You know, the Californio, the Ranch Princess, the tragic half Indian, the blue-eyed and black-haired, the sister to Spanish Felipe, the inheritor of a fallen man's jewels, the victim of Señora Moreno the America hater, the lost in the land, the widow of a mad Indian, Ramona the mother, Ramona the one you seek! Where do you find her? Spanish California! The lower, "Alta" part. The ranchos, the mission ruins, the priests, the last Days of the Dons, the New America, 1850! The days that never left. Now!

Though Ramona's fame has waned as men look to the rocket, to la frontera of the Moon and Mars, here in Southern California—Ramonaland—is where America once dreamed. For those pilgrims rusty on Ramona lore, be not ashamed, your guide, Zorro, will let you know all you need to know to enjoy this romance of Old California. With this book, you'll be a true offspring of Ramonaland, too!

The Story of Ramona!

Was Ramona fact or fiction? The passage of time, the mishmash of historical accounts, and Ramona sites and sightings springing everywhere makes the point moot. The story of California and the story of Ramona, the half-caste *Californio*, are intertwined.

Be advised that the plot of Ramona will make you as breathless as marching up Ramonaland hills. Take care when reciting her tale! Do not become the next to black out in the retelling and abandon eager neophyte ears. Don't blame your guide, Zorro, as you come to: You have been warned.

Ramona, a story was written in 1880 by Helen Hunt Jackson and popularized the *Californio* lifestyle of lariats and lace we all adore and long for. Set just after the Mexican-American war, Ramona is raised as a Mexican rancher's daughter. Her hateful mother tells her she is adopted, and Ramona learns to her delight that she is half Indian as she is in love with an Indian ranch hand named Alessandro, a pairing her mother despises. She denies Ramona her inheritance from her true father, a fallen gambler who gave Ramona to the care of Señora Moreno's departed sister. Ramona absconds from the ranch, marries Alessandro, and enters the misadventure of the Californian wilderness and frontier. Alessandro is ill-equipped for living in this American land as he goes mad, steals a horse, and meets the brutal justice of the Gringo. Ramona eventually marries her adopted brother Felipe and retires to Mexico, leaving their beloved ranch to fall in the hands of the treacherous Americans, the fate of her jewels, unknown. Whew!

Ramona's Riches

Ramona's jewels, once hidden behind her bedroom crucifix at Rancho Moreno and lost on her journey, are said to be spread throughout the state, one dropped at her every stop. Others say they never existed, and others say a horde of Ramona's treasure lies in forgotten bandit caches. Like the Forty-Niners of old, many come to California to find their fortune and failing that, find the story of Ramona and fall in love with her and the state that bore her.

While some Ramona pilgrims may sneer at your greed, any true Ramonaland scholar such as your humble author Zorro knows the jewels of Ramona mean much more than mere wealth, for if any object could claim the status of a Californian Excalibur, it would be Ramona's inheritance of jewels.

While many say this is just a dumb legend birthed in slow trains and traffic jams, who knows!

Stranger oddities exist out West.

As we all know, Ramona only claimed one small luxury from the mass wealth her father left her. Or in the bardic words of Helen Hunt Jackson and Ramona herself:

"Ramona had untied the last knot. Holding the handkerchief carefully above the tray, she shook the pearls out. A strange, spicy fragrance came from the silk. The pearls fell in among the rubies, rolling right and left, making the rubies look still redder by contrast with their snowy whiteness.

'I will keep this handkerchief,' she said, thrusting it as she spoke, by a swift resolute movement into her bosom."

While there have been many dizzying debates in scholarly circles to what *artefact d' Ramona* comprises her jewel-horde, how many artifacts must one hold before true lordship of the land is gained, to pull the sword from the stone as it were, is uncertain. Every Ramona attraction may hold a clue or will at least bring you closer to understanding Ramona. Keep looking! YOU might become the next 'King' of California.

Ramona Diary

It is an old tradition to make a travel diary about all the places visited on a trip to California. Some pilgrims say the jewels they return with are their own Ramona diaries. Not only is a Ramona Diary created to reflect upon the return to the mundane non-Californian world, but your notes create a valued clue book for jewel finding. In addition, it is beneficial to relatives to share your last moments if you are one of the many who do not make it back from your journey into the land of dreams.

Zorro's Note:

Do not eschew the traditional Ramona diary, pard! You may return home to your dugout or city condo at first happy to be alive, but then be forced to fake a diary, scribbling away to answer all those questions homebody yahoos and crackers press upon you about your trip out West. Do not rely upon faulty memory, which normally shifts events to the fantastic.

Get ready to start your own Ramona Diary, your report of wonder! Remember you can always use the margins of this very guidebook if you're missing a proper notebook from your pack. If they have already been filled in by some other Ramona-Argonaut, this book is used up and you will have to buy another. Unless, that is, you are among the rare who find the journeys of others as compelling as your own. So, follow in the footsteps of Zorro, your guide, who has followed in the footsteps of Ramona. Get to it, pard!

3.

Ramona Diary of SRD: True Son of Ramonaland

Ramona's jewels have been in the background all my life, on candy plastic rings, hidden in cereal boxes, and rumored to be underfoot. Ramona is a brand, a story, a history, a beginning of a state. Ramona is the town I grew up in. Ramona has been a label dancing on top of the land, buzzing so loud I didn't realize Ramona was my story. I didn't realize her jewels were my jewels. Until Grandma asked me to get them.

Though mostly silent on our Mission Indian heritage, grandma often told me we came from Californio Ranchers. She always said, "Don't let the gringos say you don't belong here. They don't belong." On her deathbed she asked me to do three things, believe in God (I didn't tell her I'm not religious), don't date white girls (I didn't remind her I'm half-white and bad at Spanish), and get Ramona's jewels (I didn't tell her I don't think they're real).

She then told me Ramona is our ancestor. She also told me that Ramona's jewels are a part of California and if anyone should claim them, it should be real Californios. Real natives of California. It should be us.

That moment I realized Ramona's confused mixed-race story was my own story. Once I argued with my mother about her wanting to be a hippy version of an Indian. "Why can't you be Mexican like everyone else?" Grandma said we're nothing if not Mexican. Grandpa, from New Mexico and who never said much, told us we could be what we want, but he was Spanish.

After telling me about the jewels, Grandma gave me a red silk cloth with wrinkles left by old knots and worn, small spherical impressions. Ramona's handkerchief that once held pearls. I knew from her story that it was her father's handkerchief, the only luxury Ramona wanted from her inheritance.

"Are the jewels real, Grandma?"

"We're real. We're here. We're not make-believe."

I left my grandmother so she could tell my sister and my cousin Rebecca they were her favorite like she told me, but I knew there was only one handkerchief—Ramona's and now mine.

I had been living in Texas with my white father when my grandmother passed and for years lived close to him after college. Yet, dreams about my promise never let me go. Whenever I dreamed, I dreamed of oranges, chilies, and the perturbed waves of the Pacific. Ranch houses, church bells, Mission graveyards and family house parties. Winding mountain roads and bandidos in the hills. Texas seemed worse for the dreams, flat and uninspired, but I let my promise to my grandmother slide.

Then the book came out.

The book, *True Son of Ramonaland* was written by a man who went by the name of Zorro. He gave interviews in a black shiny cape and a velvety mask, always cheap like a bad Batman costume. His book was part history, part personal story of his love of Ramona and "the period." He claimed to have the "Greatest collection of privately-owned Spanish California paraphernalia." He was an asshole who wept when Jenny asked him on the *Jenny!* talk show, "Are you the son of Ramona?" and he said, "That's what I feel in my heart." He was a white Yankee who made money by selling companies their own names on the web. He moved to California after a brief visit years ago—he was a tourist that wouldn't leave. In a theater he owned he played the old Zorro serials for kids. When they heard that the *Jenny!* the audience let out an endearing, "Awww." Jenny, herself, all smiles, asked him, "Do you have the jewels of Ramona?" Zorro slapped his chunky thigh. "I will find them." Jenny widened her famous cut-to-your-inner-light hazel eyes, "Will you?" Zorro raised his fist covered in black polyester. "I will!" The audience cheered. The camera lingered on his fist as the program faded to commercial.

I swore Zorro wouldn't see a dime from me. Luckily, I worked in a bookstore so stealing a copy was easy. As I read my stolen *True Son of Ramonaland,* I bit nearly every page. It said we *Californios* were dead (bite) and that all Americans must do what they can to preserve the bygone age of Spanish California (bite), which must be defended from "ardent Chicano revisionists" (chomp). Strangely, *True Son of Ramonaland* also gave a lot of information on Mission Indian baskets and Zorro's, "peripatetic journey collecting them," (another euphemism for robbing and swindling I was sure) but by then I lost my taste for reading and biting. Instead, I carried the old red handkerchief everywhere and pressed it hard into my eyes when I thought of my unkept promise. The spicy scent Ramona smelled was long gone and I smelled only must and rot. When I could sleep, I dreamt of my grandmother, silent.

I needed sleep. I needed dreams. I knew I needed to return to California and keep the promise I could: Stop Zorro and claim the California that is mine. Find the jewels for grandma, for me, for my dreams.

I thought about going until I was already on my way in my battered gas guzzler American car and North Texas plains turned to West Texas scrub and then to New Mexican pastel and then to deeper dryer Arizona, and then finally I was in the southwest of the Southwest, the edge of everything, the desert on a coast where I was born. Southern California. Ramonaland.

I have to keep things straight, figure everything out for myself. Though a native, I'm making my own Ramona diary, for my return to Old California. And I'm writing on the only paper I had at hand—the pages of *True Son of Ramonaland.* It's fitting I put my reality on top of Zorro's weird fantasy.

The jewels could be anywhere here, but I know they're also in my blood, in my head, in the only California that's real to me, the one I carry, the quaking California inside. But I'll find them. Because whatever there is to Ramona, fake or real, the half-caste, the Mexican American, the Californio, the Native American, the Scotswoman, it belongs to me, the (true) son of the son of the son of the son of the son of Ramona.

4.

True Son of Ramonaland: Examples of Recent Ramona Diaries

It's not always clear what tradition requires of us, especially in sunny California. To give a helpful push by example, I, your humble guide Zorro, include these excerpts from other Ramona Journals for your edification. Remember, it's okay if no one else believes what you wrote, you know it's true because you were there!

Zorro's Note:

True Son of Ramonaland caters to a wide community and concessions to the eyes of young offspring cannot always be taken into account. The California free for all is open to all, so parents read along with and prepare little Ramona Argonauts for what is to come.

Terry from the Twin Cities

I sobbed for days after finishing *Ramona*. I knew I must travel to California to tour the state to find true love, just as Ramona had.

In Ramonaland

People are so friendly here and share their food. Locals took me to see so many amazing things! A waterfall that falls backwards or upwards, rather. One guy named Hector knew the great grandson of Felipe Moreno and we saw the shack where he lives. He blessed us in Spanish and cooked us a stew of some kind. There were no cars or electricity, but I felt there was magic everywhere and I had gone back in time to the days of Ramona! Felipe's great grandson gave me a native blouse with fringe and an embroidered wolf's head on it. He said it was my spirit animal.

I kissed Hector outside in the desert night. We watched the stars and he spoke sweetly to me in Spanish. Helen Hunt Jackson herself must have gotten the same treatment from these Mexicans or Indians, whatever they are.

On reading this at home

In my suitcase all I have is a used 80s shirt with that beer drinking dog and two bimbos on it. Hector isn't in any of the photos I have—just hippy strangers in old desert sheds and ripped up teepees. What really happened? I didn't even get a Ramonaland mug.

Robert from Kansas

On starting out

The kids need to see America, to tour this grand eternal nation. Last year we did the *Scarlet Letter* New England tour, and now the wife won't shut up about Ramona this or that. I am upset about the lack of continuity: next we should do the *Last of the Mohicans* tour, then *Ramona*, then the *Gone With the Wind tour*. But what the hell, we are here.

At the Ramona Orchard

Me and the wife found an orchard and wandered about. Nothing but corn and wheat grows where we're from. I don't even know what kind of fruit was grown in the orchard, the fruit pulsated and had neon stripes. They vibrated when we tried to pick them and squirted something in little Angela's eyes. We found a hose and spent an hour getting the syrupy, stinging stuff out of her face. It was hilarious!

At the Beach

After the second day at the beach, I decided to get into the water. I had never seen the ocean and so I worried about sharks. I was treading and something latched on my side and pulled me down.

...It was Sea Indians! They told me the white man had taken all the land, so all they had left was the ocean. Breathing underwater is a trick that all Indians knew and they taught me. The chief told me the hunter thought I was a fat albino sea lion so that's why they speared me. They felt bad about it and helped me heal. I got to eat lots of fresh seafood— I don't get this at home in the Midwest. I communicated via the chief's daughter who often spoke English with surfers when they strayed too close to their underwater village.

I assumed that she loved me and that I would stay and become chief of these savages as I learned their politics and their ways, but the entire time a child had been poking me. When I finally had learned a word or two of Sea Indian, I asked him why he poked me.

"Because the princess is going to eat you fatty!"

Only then did I explore and find the surfboard tables with human skull soup bowls. Then I realized I had not only been eating fish. I grabbed a surfboard/tombstone/dinner table and swam for the surface. Many Sea Indians followed and threw spears, but the surfboard was an old wooden one that shielded my entire body.

While the Sea Indians knew the trick of breathing under water, they had forgotten the trick of breathing out of water. When they leaped up trying to grab me, I held on to one. I only let go when he thrashed and begged for water-air. Surfers sat on their boards looking at my fight. As I kicked towards the beach, I saw them dunked in the water off their boards, their curly blond heads sinking under. There were others for Sea Indians to dine on.

My family was still on the beach, wondering where the hell I had been for half an hour. They were hungry and mad. I didn't tell them about the Sea Indians, nor did they question the scar on the side of my belly, they were so focused on getting Ramona burgers.

Ramona Mission Hotel

All night I couldn't sleep. I missed the lifestyle of the Sea Indians. I missed the chief's daughter, who didn't nag, and the children there who didn't listen to rap. They wanted to eat me, but I didn't blame them. Fish and squid must get old. I filled the bathtub and sank underneath, still knowing the trick of breathing water. I drifted off to sleep, wishing to go back to the ocean. I woke up in the bedroom, EMTs shocking me back to life and my wife sobbing. It was time to go home.

Tony from Upstate New York

We stayed on the Ramona Dude ranch to have the full hardcore Ramona experience: no electronics or anything. Just my diary and the novel *Ramona*. And ranching life sucks! We got dirty water from a bucket in a well. We had to slaughter our own meat. We couldn't always find enough wood for the fire and had to use dry cow shit and the smell got into everything. The night we decided not to burn cow crap, I froze. One night a bear came up to my tent and stared. I was like I'm a tourist, dude! Ranching is hardcore, but not brutal enough for Gabe so we are going to do the Ramona Adventure Hike and then crash with Gabe's step-sister for a while.

On Hiking

We were supposed to be resting up on the Ranch for the big hardcore hike. Gabe thought we should get the full 19th century experience, and we are! I'm hardcore starving. All we have to eat is a tough horse meat jerky. Our guide is a creepy old dude who lives alone in a shack. I'm worried he's going to kill us. He keeps calling us soft like a girl. He has no teeth. Last night he said he loves us and petted our hair. He said he doesn't want to dishonor us though. Me and Gabe were scared and said, "Thanks, bro." We have no place else to go in the hardcore desert to get away.

Majella Trail

Our guide died. He was really old. It was hardcore. Gabe thought it was heart disease. No cell phone, no map because the old dude said we didn't need them. I didn't want to bury him, but Gabe did. I wish we would just ride quads in the desert like his step-sister suggested.

We kept seeing these towns and we'd start running, crying, "Praise Jah, bro, praise Jah." We get up to them and see they are like 1950s ghost towns, with nothing in them. Gabe found a candy bar, like sixty years old. Atomic Chocolate. Irradiated for preservation. We weren't low on horse jerky, but Gabe hardcore ate it.

Ramona Dress Museum and Topless bar

We weren't excited when we saw this town, thinking it was another ghost town. The only place open was the topless bar. Luckily, we have plenty of money since we had nowhere to spend it in the desert and money makes you stink less. Gabe got the "Full Ramona" and when the stripper turned around to buck on his jock, it turned out to be his step-sister! We were stoked. She was like, "Hey, it's my little brother! Don't worry, I'll get you another girl." Gabe grabbed her arm and was like, "I paid for a Full Ramona, didn't I?" and she kept on him. Hardcore! I'm eating a week-old chicken fried steak from the buffet.

Chilling at Gabe's sister's

I finally finished reading *Ramona*. I've come to understand the proud people of this area. Wish I knew what I was looking at when I was lost! We got the total Ramona experience though—we got lost, our guide-boyfriend died, we were saved by a step-sister and had hardcore monkey sex with her. I think she told Gabe some family secrets, like Felipe told Ramona about the jewels and their mom dying. I know Gabe was crying about something. Maybe just because he banged the step-sister he grew up with.

Howard from Boston

Finding the Shack

It took five years and now I am as certain as one can be dealing with a tale interlaced with fiction and reality that I found the shack where Ramona and Alessandro lived when Alessandro went mad and stole a horse. As he was shot off the stolen horse just outside the threshold, I am certain the mad Indian will haunt this nasty little shanty.

I've spent my last dime on ghost-detecting equipment. Not only will I have the unequivocal statement on the life and times of Ramona from her husband's point of view, I might gain knowledge of the whereabouts of Ramona's jewels. Even though he did not know of them in life, he is sure to have gained information which so concerned his wife in the afterworld.

My first night in the cabin

It's a long hike to the shack and I was exhausted. It's so well preserved I opened a tin of beans from the 1850s! They should be fine heated up, I hope. So far my ghost detecting equipment tells me nothing.

Day 3

My ghost needle has been jerking up and down all day. I would use my infrared video camera to be certain about a ghostly presence, but it has gone missing.

Day 8

So many things have gone missing. Last night a loud moan of, "Majella, Majella!" wouldn't let me sleep.

Day 10

All my equipment is gone. I'm stuck with the crap left in the cabin. I'm sure it's Alessandro taking my things. I sleep clutching to my remaining blanket.

Day 15

Alessandro has revealed himself as an average looking gentleman with a ghostly aura. He has no feathers or breechcloth as does every Indian of imagination, but wears rough canvas workmen's clothes of the time, save for a colorful sash. Every day is a struggle. We fight over the pan when I'm cooking my one hundred and fifty year old beans and he scoops them up in his ghost bowl as soon as they are cooked and disappears. If I try to drink, he materializes his mouth just under the nozzle of my canteen, then he steals the canteen.

He does, however, communicate with me, which would make my thirst, hunger, and irritation bearable if it weren't for one thing. He doesn't speak English. One would think that entering the infinity of the afterlife would teach one English. And make him not want to steal my belongings.

Zorro's Note:

The rescue party sent to the cabin surmised the ghost of Alessandro finally stole Howard himself, along with the last of the ancient canned beans. Only Howard's journal was left, either as a warning to those with hubris enough to search for Ramona's jewels or because Alessandro's ghost still had no interest in it as it was written in an unknown tongue for him. Or most likely, Howard was driven mad by eating canned beans from the 19th century and wandered off and joined the ranks of the many mad men who roam the California wilderness.

5.

Ramona Diary of SRD: Kicked Out of California

I got kicked out of California because I asked for a ride down the street. The week before at football practice, someone's red helmet went under my vision and then red rocketed into my hip. I got up and limped. Then limped everywhere, limped home, limped at school, limped at practice where the pain felt like being stuck with a red tabasco flavored spear. We didn't have money for the doctor. I put up with it. At home I limped to the bathroom and fell to the floor, unable to put any weight on my right leg. Elvis dying on the toilet was the first thing I can remember seeing on TV, along with a visual representation of the mountain of drugs he did. "Not like Elvis!" My brain repeated and I dragged myself to our leftover nice couch from our nice house that now served in our crappy apartment in the crappy part of Ramona, the town. Mom came in and screamed, "Get up you lazy shit," as she normally did. When she saw I was hurt, she called me a faker until my sister backed me up by saying it looks real. Then mom said what I already knew. "We don't have no money for the goddamn doctor so just be a goddamn man about it."

A couple days later, Dad called and said in his now stronger than ever Texas accent that I should, "Go to the doctor, buddy." Buddy? I was never a buddy before. He somehow got whiter. Mom took me only after talking to dad on the phone a bunch before she changed reality. "I say go to the doctor and you don't go. Your father tells you to go and then you go. I see how you kids hate me."

Mom was crazy, that was life. When we lived in the big house in the Estates outside of town, Mom would crash into my room and slap me and growl and yank up my hair and run out. Then minutes later her friends would be over-sneering and disapproving before their séance or the hippy burn outs would tell her, the only Native person in the group, about native wisdom. Or she'd come in and terrorize constantly for the two to four weeks dad was on business trips. She'd smash things or slap me over some minor infraction (always reported on the phone to dad: Mark, Scott got a B, Mark, Scott left a dish out!) but still would say wait until your father gets home. Once I rubbed my face and said, "Shit, I wish he was home." Mark, Scott is cursing. Dad would come home with his WASPy 1950s *Leave It To Beaver* "Hi, hi!" sitcom hello. "Mark, Mark, your son…" He'd sigh and tell me to go to my room and then come in later and say he missed me and, "Yer momma is mad. Are you sorry?" "Sorry? For real? Dad, mom is crazy and a liar."

He'd only say, "Yer momma is tired." "Tired? She wakes me up in the middle of the night to tell me I'm stupid." Once I screamed look at my books! Mom regularly ripped my books. I repaired them with tape and precision and I always kept books friends lent me hidden under the bed. "Why would I rip up my own books!" Dad would only be silent. Or say, "Were you able to fix it?"

I was kicked out because of the argument mom and I had in the car, but it wasn't that. I was probably kicked out because I had grown larger and stronger than her. She refused to see it at first though. As we tore up the falling apart backyard to sell the big house in the Estates, I started pulling up the awful glued on plastic green rug. Mom said just goddamn drop that, you are too weak. I tugged and pulled up half of it. "What?" "Your son is becoming a man, Polly," my Aunt Linda said with pride. Mom gasped, worried. My time in that house, or any house with her, was numbered from then.

My sister Clara and I had stayed indoors all that summer in hotter than even the desert we lived in Dallas, Texas. We spent weekends at BBQs with Uncle Billy Bob and Aunt Sonya and dealt with his practical jokes of hiding a radio under dad's bed. Dad's crazy half-drunk teacher girlfriend was nice. My sister was angry at me for being nice back. "It's bad for mom!"

That summer was the most latch key kids existence we ever had. All day just inside. We watched *Alice. One day at a time. Brady Bunch* (oh

Marsha, Marsha, Marhsa). *MASH* which my sister hated. And tons of *Happy Days* which always confused me…a 50s fantasy perpetually in that decade, the characters never dealing the cultural watershed of the 60s yet everyone aged, and everyone and everything was so 1970s even more so than I could remember because I mostly ran and played and bounced window to window in the backseat of giant cars without a seat belt. And got slapped.

We flew back at the end of summer and met mom at the airport. My sister ran up and said, "Mommy!" They hugged and mom looked at me and grunted. "You came back." I didn't hug her at all.

By then we lived in town in a dilapidated apartment in a complex where all the broke Mexicans lived. I ignored my home life. I got yelled at but not slapped.

Now, one of my best friends in the Estates thought he was too cool for me, which hurt and was odd—he was the biggest nerd in junior high and everyone still saw him as such, though he grew out his hair and dropped acid. My other friend Jay had spent the summer driving and drinking and making a new best friend, less nerdy. D&D wasn't cool, which we knew, but he didn't have any interest in it anymore. Don't mention *Star Trek*, the choice of abject dorks, around his new best friend. The new best friend worked at Safeway and was able to get hard booze, not like the cheap beer that we normally paid undocumented guys to buy us in the Estates. Jay and the new best friend did small town teenage stuff, like riding the hoods of cars as they drank and drove down big hills and dirt roads. I did a few of these things with them, but I sensed I wasn't welcome, and time hanging with them would end. My white friends from the estates had all started slumming. I had no choice anymore living in the bad part of town. They hung out with people they called white trash, and talked about joining the military like them, but most of them had the additional option of working for dad. I wasn't their neighbor nor a true slum friend for them.

I wore my great uncle's army jacket and put pins all over it instead of dressing like a preppy like my popular sister demanded. The school moved me to honors classes and in every class was the girl I loved since 7th grade. And I wasn't the only smart kid in class anymore, but I was the only Mexican or Indian besides her.

Though it was the high desert the mist that formed over the night doesn't always burn off in the morning. We had London level fog sometimes. You could get snatched by Jack the Ripper or someone who looked like Charles Manson since this was California. In this misty morning I beat and swam over the offensive tackles eyeing the quarterback and as always expected there to be another back to bash me, but maybe there were twins, or maybe it was the quarterback. That's when someone's helmet speared me in the hip.

I didn't have a car. I walked everywhere. I limped. It hurt like hell, but I played all week and went to school. If I rested a day or two at first it wouldn't have been that bad. Getting kicked out might have happened a month later, even.

My friend's new best friend helped me cross lines as we sprinted in practice, but we didn't talk much. He was embarrassed to be seen with me. I was probably the only Brown person he was ever friends with.

I went to the doctor, who just said take it easy, no walking around. And the day after I asked for a ride to take me to practice. Even though we moved to town from our big house in the Estates and lived only a couple of blocks from school, it was still too far to limp there. Mom kept telling me to walk, and I said, please, mom, it would only take a minute. It was just two blocks away.

In the car, she kept saying, "Why do you even go? You'll just hurt yourself again, and I'll have to fucking drive you. Walk next time, you lazy shit."

She had always taken my sister everywhere she needed without complaints. While I didn't expect, of course, any quality mother-son time that I never had, I just got back from staying in Texas for the summer. Ignoring the lunatic insults had stopped working. I was out of practice, though she had already cussed me that morning, that afternoon, and right then.

"I can't walk, you idiot, that's why I asked for a ride."

"You talk to your mother like that?"

"You talk to me like that all the time! You can't even spare two minutes for your own son."

She started swinging the car this way and that like a maniac until she parked on the dirt by the school, still screaming though other kids were close by.

"I was hoping you wouldn't come back. Why'd you come back? Just go live with your goddamn father."

I punched the glovebox and made the door fling out and show the stuffed insides of fast food receipts, maybe tickets, maybe important documents along with gum wrappers, and probably my birth certificate.

"Fine," I said, "Have fun telling grandma and grandpa you kicked your son out."

Mom was quiet, but just before I got out and slammed the car door that I thought might fall off, she said,

"You think they love you? No one does."

I hobbled over to football practice, coaches already shouting, "Duncan, you're late!" and thought I should have gotten kicked years ago. Getting kicked out was easy.

I came home later and she sat there like a laconic Olmec panda and acted as if she had come to a wise decision instead of fighting with me. She told me I was leaving next week and, "It's for the best, m'ija," forgetting to say "oh" rather than "ah" as always and began playing the old wise suffering mother. "It's m'ijo, cah-bron-ah." I hoped that was the last thing she'd ever hear from me.

The funny thing was school seemed better than ever just before I was leaving. My favorite wrestling coach had just become the defense football coach. I was finally in advanced History and English and out of advanced Math (I was good at something I hated). I had finally fought back enough against Anglo assholes that called me beaner so that getting punched was a rare event.

Yet oddly, when I finally told everyone I was moving, everyone was indifferent. My sister seemed distant, as always. I focused on moving to Dallas, a big city, where no one knows you and doesn't give a shit and being away from this redneck high mountain town, where everybody knows you, hates you, and doesn't give a shit.

A week later, I still limped. I liked the small-town Ramona football games, it was more of a social event and no one cared about watching the game, really. I was leaving the next day. My friends, who were engrossed with the freedom of the roads and boozing, didn't even hang out with me much last night.

I bumped into the girl I liked who was in all my honors classes and told her I was leaving. In the half dark between the over bright field and the fluorescent light flowing out from the concessions stand window, she looked worried and gave me a hug. She wrote her address on my hand and said to keep in touch. She knew about the divorce and the move to town—all the family shame. For once it seemed someone actually knew about what was going on with me. At that moment, I was sure she liked me, though I was terrified and felt I wasted time since junior high not telling her I liked her. It was late and I was getting a ride with my sister's friend. The natural arena, the pit of the stadium, was a microcosm of the town. The redneck 4H types segregated from the preppy country club people from my old neighborhood, and of course, from anyone Mexican. I felt happy to leave. In the restroom I was going to wash my hands and face and I stared at the address. A month before I would have been giddy to have even this connection, this mark, the reminder how she held my arm to steady my upturned palm as she wrote her number.

My hands went under the faucet—I wanted a new start in the big city of Dallas. She would be something to hold me to the town and in my teenage mind I thought I'd be free of small-town hate, the border, being once too rich, now too poor, being too white, being too Mexican, too American Indian, too whatever, and most of all…

…free of Ramona forever.

6.

True Son of Ramonaland: Pulp Ramona

Here Zorro includes Ramona related stories of interest from the golden age of magazines—entertainment when the word was not competed with by television or iPods or the pictorial laden internet. As so often for travelers, batteries run out, lines become too long, or the wilderness becomes too big. Allow these interludes to entertain you for when the factual accounts on Ramonaland history becomes too dull or for those times when words escape your pen for your Ramona Diary. Dream of Ramona as our grandparents did, freed from the constraints of her own story and tramping into others.

As your guide, Zorro does not own the rights to these tales, I can only summarize them for your potential enjoyment at a later date for when the full stories are procured at a fine bookseller.

1. *Ramona on Mars*

Ramona, separated from Alessandro, enters an old Indian cave while wandering California looking for a place to live away from brutish American thieves. An ancient green mist rises and lulls her to unconsciousness. The mist transports her to Mars. Much stronger than the average Martian, Ramona roams naked and becomes a leader of men. Soon the whole of Mars fears her as Majella, warrior woman. When, years later, a luckless American wanders to the same mysterious cave, she has him killed but not before he gives her a child, the first human born on Mars—a boy named Alessandro.

2. Ramona in Hell

Ramona fights the devil over her baby. The devil demands her to meet his challenge on the fiddle, but Ramona tells him she can only sing. The devil agrees and Ramona sings a song about Jesus which burns the devil's ears. Ramona jabs the cross upon her neck into his chest. She snatches her swarthy baby and runs out back to California. The devil still cries in agony from the cross stuck in his breast and quakes California when the pain becomes too great.

3. The Pirate-ess Ramona

After the death of her husband Alessandro, Ramona loses faith in humanity and joins a band of motley pirates. The pirates fall in love with her simple ways and they raid the California and Mexican coast for ships laden with gold. Zorro sneaks upon her ship to disable it and bring this pirate queen to justice. Ramona awakens, with Spanish and Indian blood enraged, and duels the Fox, only to receive a mortal blow. Ramona repents in Zorro's arms and he removes his mask—only for her—and plants a kiss as she dies.

4. The Rage of Ramona

Ramona loses her mind after Alessandro dies and becomes a serial killer, luring American gringos to their doom. She lingers in saloons, drinking whiskey, exposing a leg, and leads by hand unsuspecting white men to shadowy alleys. She kisses them, tells them of her husband. The men invariably ask, "This wild injun ya married ta, he ain't around is he?" Loco-eyed Ramona laughs and flings her hair. "No, no he is gone. Gone from this world," and she draws her assassin stiletto. She kisses and jabs, no mind for blood on her red and black dress. The story ends imploring care upon the reader in dealings with these seductive and vengeful Mexicans.

5. The Good Mormon and Ramona

A Good Mormon explains to Ramona that the ancestors of her and her Indian husband are not the original inhabitants of the New World, but the murderers of the blessed white natives whom Jesus appeared to. The truth of the book of Mormon terrifies Alessandro and he steals a horse to trample the Good Mormon who shoots the skin-cursed-by-god Indian before it is too late. Thankfully Ramona attempts to seduce the Good Mormon with coffee and sex, but the Good Mormon rides off to report her to the elders.

6. Rebel Ramona

Ramona's anger over Alessandro never leaves her. The Americans steal the last of the Moreno Ranch, Felipe becomes a broken man. Ramona wanders the wilderness as she did with Alessandro so long ago. She comes upon the bandit cave of Joaquin Murrieta, who falls in love and dubs her the bandit queen. The whole of Southern California quakes in terror as they burn American house upon American house, gaining anti-American supporters along the way until finally the roused combined might of the common citizenry and US Army rides out and to face them.

7. Ramona, the Coyote

Ramona must have forgotten something as she comes back to the US again and again, but this time with friends! The border patrol shook their fingers at her and sent her back smiling.

7.

True Son of Ramonaland: Bandit Hideout of Joaquin Murrieta

Background:

While decapitated by Ranger Captain Harry Love, Joaquin Murrieta lives on through his bandit underlings who swarm California and ply their illicit trade. Information on Mexican criminal activities is delivered nightly through local news stations for your safety. Here, most sordid of all places, a bauble or two of Ramona's are sure to be found yet are equally sure to be inaccessible. Do not stray from the Ranger station, the gateway to the desert wilderness of canyons and coyotes—no Captain Love will be able to save you from the evil of *bandido* whims.

Things to do:

It is ill-advised to seek bandit gold or attempt to be compensated for an encounter with one of these Mexican banditti. Rape, robbery, foul language, and death are the probable outcomes if you stray from the marked path and come face to face with the likes of Joaquin Murrieta and his foul Mexican horde.

Zorro's Note:

While they are colorful, entertaining, and raucous, the *bandidos* of California are not associated with any entertainment organization and are NOT ACTORS. They are very real and exist outside the law. Your valuables, even your body, may not be yours any longer. Prepare for the worst, the author of this guide cannot be held responsible for the effects of your misguided curiosity.

8.

The Ramona Diary of SRD: The Head Joaquin

Is Joaquin real? Some say yes. Folk hero to the Chicanos of California, the Californios, yet murderous bandit leader to Anglos, he had his story told in an eponymous 19th century novel just like Ramona, the other Californio myth. Was Joaquin Murrieta beheaded in 1853 and put on display until lost in the Great Earthquake of 1906? Is either he or Ramona real? I asked that question when Grandma asked me to get Ramona's jewels, so central to her story. She told me, "Por cierto, all us Californios are real." But I wasn't so sure then. Now, after reading both the *Life and Adventures of Joaquin Murrieta* by the reporter John "Yellow Bird" Rollin Ridge and *Ramona, a story* by the activist Helen Hunt Jackson, I have ideas:

My Theories About Joaquin Murrieta

1. Joaquin Murrieta is dead. Captain Harry Love really decapitated him. Or…

2. Joaquin Murrieta is a mantel, a title for a bandit lord. Or…

3. Joaquin Murrieta escaped his so-called capture. He'll be old, but California's good weather keeps everyone going. And/or…

4. Joaquin is Felipe Moreno, supporting character and step-brother/husband to Ramona. Perhaps he inherited his mother's hatred of Americans and the disenfranchisement of Californios enough to turn to banditry. The man, after all, who put Ramona's jewels, my birthright, away for safety before they became lost to history, lost to us Californios. Felipe Moreno, Joaquin Murrieta, the man I need to see.

Every bandit wants his story told. Or in Joaquin's case, retold. I'll tell him I'm Yellow Bird the reporter, another half-breed like myself, doing a rewrite of *Life and Adventures.* An update. Hopefully, I won't die.

My Audience with the Head Joaquin

I eventually caught up with the elusive bandido, the Robin Hood of California, Joaquin Murrieta after many inquiries, news reports, and by the method of last resort: shutting my eyes and placing my thumb on an antiquated map of California in a psychic remote viewing technique, which led to a burning hacienda. I should say I had caught up with his men who sat on the veranda drinking liquor and waiting on who-knows-what while the flames chewed at the back of the house and topped the roof.

I parked just before them and stepped out of my car with the smashed-in side, my Ramona Diary at the ready. As I called out, "Hola, fellows," they used the famous Californio lariat and I was caught around the neck and yanked to the ground. In shock, I was unable to state my purpose and display my faux credentials as a man of letters. My shock compounded as they proceeded to prepare me for an unspeakable act, far too common out here on the western frontera. Spitting out blood to state my purpose was ineffectual, so I resorted to swallowing blood and was finally able to shout, "I'm John Rollin Ridge! Yellow Bird! I'm here to write another story on Joaquin!"

After a short translation and deliberation among the merry band, I was released and my shorts returned to me. A man who had stayed on a rocker on the veranda and absently viewed my desperate perdition rose and came slowly down the steps. A headband under his hat, long black hair, sharp nose, and a wild Anglo-hating look, he was the Joaquin Murrieta of legend. He confirmed his identity as he stated, "Weak yanqui, I am Joaquin."

I struggled to stand, pulling up my drawers. "Dear sir! It is an honor to meet you! I am here to set straight your tale. Know that I am not a mere yanqui; as you are yourself, I am a true son of California, descendant of Spanish Rancheros. Well, also Scottish…."

"They're all the same," he said.

"Who are all the same?" I remembered his love of justice and equality.

"All those damn whites are the same."

This caused me to believe Murrieta was Indian after all. Or an angry, confused Mestizo (as if there are any other kinds of half-breed). My theories about him burned as fierce as the hacienda.

I remembered my cover as John Rollin Ridge. I pulled my Ramona Diary and pencil from the dust. "Sir, could you tell me your tale, starting from your encounter with Captain Harry Love?"

He looked at me. "I am not that Joaquin."

"What?"

"Which Joaquin do you mean? There are many."

Another man, the filthy and massive heathen who sought to assault my honor, said, "I am Joaquin, too."

A few other men asserted in Spanish that they were also Joaquin and they pointed out a body on the ground, stripped of boots and pants, "That guy there, he was a Joaquin."

"So who do you mean, pendejo?" Rocking Chair Joaquin said.

"Mur… Murrieta. Joaquin Murrieta."

Rocking Chair Joaquin sneered. "Oh. Him. Yeah."

The men behind me all let out, "Oh, Murrieta."

Rocking Chair Joaquin turned from me and drew his machete.

"I will take you to him, Sr. Yellow Bird, after we are done helping the people." Here, he gestured to the bloodied, dying men and recoiling women I neglected to mention earlier. "But you pissed me off by not saying you wanted Murrieta up front, so you will have a c_____s." It is an abhorrent word in Spanish, and I experienced the full depth of its meaning. It suffices to say I was beaten. Terribly beaten.

As Rocking Chair Joaquin had said, after his band had "aided" the people of the *hacienda*, we set off to see Murrieta. While blindfolded with a feed sack for days on the back of a mule, I could hear them rob liquor stores, brutalize and ravish ladies, torment a captured Highway patrolman, and have a prolonged shootout with a posse or SWAT in which several Joaquins fell. During the flight from this posse, no food, nor drink (water would be out of the question as these bandidos only quench their thirst with whiskey) came to me till the 4th day when Rocking Chair Joaquin stuffed some roasted beast in my mouth despite my protest of the cleanliness of his hands (which I knew were awful, blindfold or no) and my staunch vegetarianism and reliance on mainly grains, beans, and corn. I ate the gamey flesh, though. This dead animal, I mourn.

During this time a man with three fingers often prodded me, and though I thought it the same giant savage who assaulted me before, I recalled my Californio lore gained from *The Life and Adventures of Joaquin Murrieta.* I called out, "Three-fingered Jack, is that you?" The groping stopped, silence followed. Then I was kicked in the ear with a boot. Someone said, "Seven-fingered Joaquin, cabrón."

Additionally, they had my digital camera that I wore for the show to seem more like the reporter Yellow Bird. When they at once tackled me from the corner of my vision I saw the already dead batteries fly out. Yet a small, crooked Joaquin wore the lanyard around his neck and snapped pretend photos with the dead camera at their many group posing and of their more degenerate activities, which I'll overlook. It was during these moments of pretend photo posing that I got to scrawl out some words as the Joaquins' attention was elsewhere and the small crooked Joaquin insisted I scribble down in this diary to provide further record of their good times.

Finally, after many days and panics, the feed sack was pulled off my head and I saw that we had arrived at the bandit palace—an entrance to a cave with an ornate oak door torn from some residence and affixed to a makeshift wall. The door depicted griffins in flight and bare breasted Amazons in battle: a fantasy world for an equally fantastic portal. In the middle of the depicted melee someone had carved a "J." To further seem more like a reporter, I quickly sketched it, pictured here:

J

Rocking Chair Joaquin to my surprise, explained:

"When he saw that movie about him, he made us put J's on the walls for a while. I tried to do it with a machete, but it don't work so good." Rocking Chair Joaquin gripped me and drew me to his face. "If he asks, we still draw J's."

Soon, I was inside the cavernous gloom. My feet kicked through pizza boxes, empty whiskey bottles, crushed menudo tins, and the piled gold dust of a thousand robberies, the worth of which could not match even one of Ramona's jewels due to their historical and cultural significance, including the promise I made to grandma to get them. Deep underground, a Joaquin parted decayed curtains and we entered the bandit emperor's chambers.

Splayed on tasseled cushions and broken-down couches, mustachioed Joaquins pawed an array of gaudily painted women, some in low cut jeans exposing their midriff and others in frilly dresses that just showed a shocking amount of ankle. The sight of the women reminded me of my Murrieta and Ramona connection theory: The possibility that Murrieta was in reality Don Felipe Moreno, Ramona's own adopted brother and husband, excited my step, though later, due to unsavory circumstances, I forgot to ask.

"Well, there he is, yanqui." Rocking Chair Joaquin gesticulated towards a large glass jar on a red velvet covered table. A dead man's head was inside the jar, filled with a sepia liquid.

The ne'er-do-wells lounging about grunted amusement in their fugue and the Joaquins who had brought me all this way, guffawed so roughly that I feared and wondered at their reasons to bring me to view this monstrosity. Was this to be my fate at the hands of these desperados, to become a head in a jar? Were the Anglo tabloids correct? Were my Mexican brethren incorrigible ruffians, with no thoughts or concerns other than murder, torture, and buggery? More importantly, would I never find my illustrious ancestor-ess, Ramona? Would I never claim my inheritance of jewels, baubles, silks, and who knows what else? I slid to my knees in terror of the debauched laughter surrounding me and my presumed dark fate.

"*Shab-UB!*" the dead man's head sloshed in the jar and called out.

My brain twisted. I choked at the air, full of drug smoke and the scent of long unwashed flesh. The bandidos and harlots ceased their noise. Dust from the cave roof above us settled to the once precious and now tattered rugs below. What man could silence such lowlifes as these Joaquins, other than their chieftain? He was THE Joaquin among the Joaquins. Scourge of the Yankees, Mexican Robin Hood, Californio resistance fighter—nay savior. He was Joaquin Murrieta, and he was a head in a jar.

Though the truth of his appearance as an animate, swelled, gray head in amber fluid unsettled me, I introduced myself as Yellow Bird and slowly drew out my Ramona Diary and pencils, which like my theories, had broken into many pieces.

Head Joaquin interrupted, "*Bello Bab*?" through the fluid.

I told him I wanted to talk about rebooting the franchise. Head Joaquin banged against his jar. "*Borro! Borro!*" Joaquins drew their machetes and my life again was in peril as I swore I had nothing to do with Zorro, and in fact I meant to say, "Sequel." A sequel to let the world know what came after *The Life and Adventures of Joaquin Murrieta*. The real Joaquin of today. The idea enchanted him, and me as well, so much so it was here I forgot to ask about Ramona. I instead asked him what liquid he floated in.

"*Wizbee,*" he grunted and bubbled.

I asked him to shortly state his encounter with Captain Harry Love, a roundabout way to address the blaring question on my mind, that is, how did he truly end up in a jar? I assumed the head paraded around our state, much like defeated Vercingetorix before Rome, was not his, but some other unfortunate suspiciously Mexican. I believe he told me the truth, but the sounds he made, "*Swoosh boosh wulb, gluk gluk, weeb mop gah,*" were more akin to the noises of a drowning man than words. I feigned a transcription and rose as I wrote, rising to one knee and then resting on the worn velvet of the tablecloth. I was inches from the famous man. We have all seen the newsreels and wanted posters, describing a man 5'5" to 6'7", an Indio or Mestizo, along with conflicting reports that he was a landed Criollo (and hence my Don Moreno theory). Descriptions so vague that every Mexican of California is a suspected Joaquin Murrieta.

To ever learn about Ramona, to learn about Joaquin, the real Joaquin, I realized that I would have to pull him out of the whiskey to truly hear him. Head Joaquin continued his drowning man cacophony, "*Blurb, slup slup, woo baek. Ah ah*!" and the plan formulated in my mind which since has reshaped my life: the plan that caused me to live hated by both those within the law and those without it.

The desperados partook of the pipe or the low women, so my transcribing was sometimes halted by a drug induced night terror, or too loud an impassioned yelp. While they were thus busy and inattentive, I hefted up Head Joaquin's jar as he was lost in reminiscence, babbling and bubbling on and on. As I passed a couch where some sexed pumping was occurring, I bumped the supine woman's leg. My jacket button snagged upon her tattered stocking, pulling it off and fastening it to me. Her eyes turned from her criminal lover and I saw her blue eyes floating in her bronze face as I crept by. I wonder to this day if she was, if anyone ever was, the real Ramona, and that I gripped the wrong treasure in my hands as I left that cursed and ancient cavern. That said, I have no regret for my choice of Joaquin. As I passed through the heavy curtain she began calling, "Joaquin! Joaquin!" I made it to the main cavern alive and assumed that her screams for the Joaquin in my hands were taken for yelps of love for the Joaquin on top of her. I kicked up cans and gold dust with my inarticulate load unharmed and pushed through the fantastic gate to the mule outside, and a chance to hear the real story, the tale of California, the story of Joaquin.

9.

True Son of Ramonaland: Fernando's *Ramona* Testimonial

Indeed *Ramona, a story* has meant much to many. We include these testimonials not only to express and share the enthusiasm for *Ramona,* but to inform and iterate the weightiness and importance of this book in our lives. After all, reading *Ramona, a story* has healed the sick and the book itself has even saved lives. Unbelievable? Read these interviews of old timers and their experiences reading *Ramona* and what it has meant to them.

Testimonial One, Fernando G., LA native:

"Yeah, I was a zoot suiter, but only for one night, that last night. I didn't read the news or anything, I just saved and saved up until I could get a zoot suit like my cousin. I wanted something that would pop out, really make the girls want to dance with me, because I was a little skinny back then. My cousin Teddy had a dark blue one and my friend Johnny had a striped one, so I was going to get a purple one. I went to the guy and pointed at the cloth I wanted. The suit guy kept saying, 'You sure? Why not get a red one?' I got mad and said, 'I came in knowing what I wanted, who do you think I am?' I didn't say I'm colorblind and wouldn't know a red from green because I didn't trust that guy so much. I didn't want to walk in the dance hall like Mexican Robin Hood, you know.

Well, I got ready to go dancing with my cousin Teddy, not that we'd dance together, but our moms told us we shouldn't go out alone these days, if at all. Like I said, I didn't read the news. My cousin

Teddy never said anything, he was Sr. Toughguy and so he honked and I was running out. Mom was sitting in the dark praying like she did all the time, scaring the hell out of me and said to wear your father's hat, because I didn't have any hat and it was cold. I didn't want to argue or hear her bark about wasting money on my new suit so I grabbed dad's old cowboy hat and Teddy laughed when he saw it when I got in his car. Dad put a bunch of old feathers all over it to cover the holes, so almost the whole hat was covered. I was going to take it off for sure when I got to the club, the Charley Horse, I think. No, it was El Jefe. El something. Anyways when we were parking we yelled at some cute girls and I forgot to leave it in the car.

I got into El Something and went up to the first girl I saw, not seeing she was with some *cholo*. So I said, 'Wanna dance, doll?' like in the movies. And she says, 'I don't think so.' I take her hand and say, 'Come on sugar.' She jerked it back and said, 'I don't dance with no faeries.' Just then I remembered my hat and snatched it off, thinking she thought I was some country guy. 'What faerie?' Then the guy next to her, who was posing in a dark suit and white hat, pretended to brush my shoulder and said, 'The faerie in this pink suit, *cabrón*.' I don't really remember but –I'll get to *Ramona* in a minute, jeez, it's connected. What do you guys say, smoke some pills? And no, boys didn't wear no pink back then, smart guy—Anyways, I get real scared like, but still hoping pink isn't the truth and I laugh at him, and say, 'What are you colorblind, Jack? It's purple.' Then the girl and her friends and the guy all laugh, saying pink. Then they say it slowly in Spanish, RO-SA-DO, as if I didn't know what pink was in English. I was burning, and didn't know what to do. And I saw the girl was really pretty when she stood and that made it worse. I thought of a movie I don't know and said, 'This is the new style, Jack,' and tugged down on my lapels. They all laughed, like twisting in their seats and I was swatting people touching my zoot suit and pointing things out with their hands.

I got out of there mad and, what you say, indignant. I had no idea where my cousin Teddy was and I was mad at him too for not saying anything. He knew I was colorblind. Also, I was mad at my mom for praying in the dark. If she used one candle she would have said, '*M'ijo*, don't go out looking like no faerie,' and I wouldn't have been laughed at. So I was walking home and the next thing is that these white guys in white were calling after me. I thought I made a wrong turn, so I walked in a different direction. They kept calling, 'Hey Paco!' And I kept walking. Then they said, 'Hey, Fernando!' And I stopped because that's my name. 'Whaddaya want?' I said. Then they started charging and I turned to run but see these other white guys standing there with these white girls pointing at me, saying, 'There's one, there's a beaner.' The sailor guys caught up to me and grabbed me and I tried to stand straight and sound tough so I said, 'Unhand me, Jack,' like in that movie, but then they were all punching. They also made rips and started tearing my pink zoot suit. I was on the ground and they were ripping off my sleeve and kicking and I told you guys I didn't read the news right? Well, I thought they were after faeries, not Mexicans that day, so I shouted, 'I'm colorblind, I'm colorblind!' All those white people were laughing at me too, but still kicking me in the head. I sat up a bit and this nerd reporter took my picture. The one my mom saw in the paper with my head all bruised and blood on the street. The thing is my pink zoot suit looked white on the paper, so not so many people found out I was fighting in the street in pink clothes. Anyways, I wanted to throw a punch, but instead I lay down. When I got up, I was in a jail cell with a bunch of other Mexicans in ripped up zoot suits. I go to the bars and say to the officer "I would like to report a crime" and the cops all start laughing.

That judge didn't laugh. He preached about excesses like we were in church and about my people and all this crap. He said I could go to jail, go back to Mexico though I told him I was born here like my grandparents or be a real American and go overseas and fight the Fascists. By then the Fascists weren't the ones I wanted to fight, but I said, ok.

Next thing I know I'm stuck training with guys like the ones who beat me up. Before I left—now we get to *Ramona*, you happy? You need to relax. The doctors say being tense all the time isn't good for you. That's what they tell me anyway. My mom didn't want me to go and she wanted to give me something to keep me safe, but didn't want to give me her Bible because she said what if I lose it. So she gave me this book she was reading, *Ramona.* I said I don't read trash like that, but she tells me it's about Los Angeles and it might make me remember home. The good thing in the army is that they give you comic books, so I didn't have to read it, but she was right, I kept it with me, more because I could remember her giving it to me and that she kept it on the table with her glasses.

So in Europe lots of those what you call Anglo guys weren't happy about serving with a Mexican so to be nice I told them I was Italian and that did me good for a while but then they wanted me to interrogate some Italians and my Spanish isn't so good and not really Italian, so the prisoners were laughing at me like everyone and the white guys got mad again and so I got all the bad duties, like scouting. I kept telling them, I make a bad scout, that I got lost in Los Angeles and I lived there all my life, but they made me a scout and what-do-you-know, I got lost.

There was rubble and dark woods and no one around. I finally saw this fire and thought maybe everyone moved camp, but I walked up and there were three Germans, the first ones I ever saw. They looked like other white guys to me but all crazy like they've been fighting the war by themselves all those years. Well, one was a little kid with a nice uniform, he looked new. They made me sit down, shouting German things and the kid kept the rifle on me while the other two went through my pack and ate my chocolate and threw my stuff and stopped when they found *Ramona*. They said Ramona but in German and sat down. I don't speak German so I had to guess what they were saying, but I guess they were talking about the old days before the war and got really sad. Then they point at the cover and point at me, and I never noticed it before but the Indian guy with Ramona looked just like me. They really liked that and handed the book to me. I know I'm dark, but geez. So, I kept saying Mexican, but they weren't having that. They gabbed more about the good old days and then I saw the kid wasn't happy. He was shaking his fist and sounded like that guy, you know, Hitler, and I knew what guys like him were saying about us back then. He was a nasty little kid and I saw he made up his mind to shoot me and I wasn't having that so I threw *Ramona* spine-first at what you call it, his noggin, you know his head. So he started crying and the other guys started laughing and took his gun. They gave me my book back and then talked a bit. Then it was either the kid being nasty, tasting the chocolate and hoping to get more, or me looking like Ramona's boyfriend, I don't know which, but they gave up. They told me 'No fight, no fight.' And handed the rifle to me. I left the kid there since he was crying and kept shaking when I tried to pick him up and then he ran off. Lucky for me, the Germans knew exactly where the American camp was. I was proud of contributing to the war and capturing two guys by myself. While they were in camp I read Ramona aloud to them and the other prisoners. The other guys didn't like it, but then the captain says, 'Hey, try to get intel from them, Paco,' and their English was getting better and so I became like a top interrogator for a while, just reading to them and asking them now and then about guns and how many guys were left. I told them they didn't have to tell me anything, but it would help because we could keep reading. So, yeah, *Ramona* saved my life in the war, you know the whole thing."

10.

Ramona Diary of SRD: Scott Is A Chicano Name

Everyone had to have a Spanish name in our high school class. The Johns became Juans and all the Janes became Juanas. The few Manuels and Margaritas got to stay the same. All these kids had it easy. Then the teacher came to me.

"What's your name?"

"Scott."

"There isn't a cognate. You have to choose a Spanish name."

"I'm Chicano, so it's a Chicano name."

"No, it isn't. Your last name isn't a Latin name either. What part of Mexico are you from?"

"I got my last name from my white dad. My mom's side is from California and New Mexico."

"That's not Mexico."

"We were before the US invaded."

"Well, there isn't a word for Scott in Spanish."

"My grandma calls me Escott."

The teacher sighed.

"What's your middle name?"

"Russell."

"Didn't your parents want to give you a Latino name?"

"There are already two Juan Bautistas in the family."

"Just go by Ruse, then."

"What does that mean, Russian?"

"Close enough to Russell and you need a Spanish name for class."

I didn't want to be called Russian, it was the Cold War in the 1980s after all, but she had already moved on to the next, less difficult kid.

I had to go by Ruse, which I later found out is just a meaningless sound equivalent to Russell.

In college, the professors and TA's asked me for my Spanish name. Except when I said Scott, they would say, didn't I have Spanish in high school? What name did I use? I said, "Ruse, but it doesn't mean anything."

They told me it didn't mean anything and I said I'm Chicano so I wanted to use my own name.

And of course they said Scott isn't a Chicano name and each semester I had to go by a name I never bothered to remember because I was insistent to use my own name.

The professors encouraged the few students with Spanish last names, yet sought me out, and shamed me for every answer I didn't have. When the white students copied off my papers, they acted as if I asked Cody, I mean Carlos, to not-so-slyly lean over and copy the answer to the question about Dia de Los Muertos, a holiday my family didn't, perhaps ever, celebrate.

The head of the department was rude, had a raspy Spanish voice, and always told me to drop when I asked for help. When my paternal grandfather was dying and I asked her just outside the door of class before a test if I could talk to her, she curtly said no. I went in and cussed her out in front of everybody—en español. Unfortunately, she was the head of the department, and I had to wait till someone else taught the last class I needed. Finally, a professor offered the class and she was not just from New Mexico, but the same county as my maternal grandfather. I said, "I wanted to use Scott" even though it isn't a Spanish name. She said "Okay, it's your name," and that her son's name didn't have a Spanish cognate either. She was polite and chatted with me outside of class and though I was a struggling average student, never made me feel ashamed. She told me about meeting Borges. Best of all, she let me put Scott on my papers.

My last paper was to be on "our favorite work of art or literature." I chose Borges, "Garden of Forking Paths," as I'm a sucker for permutations and alternate outcomes. I worked hard because the section on the subjunctive kicked my ass and I had to make up for that bad grade. I wrote and wrote. I asked all my Mexican American friends, and as I suspected, their accent was better than mine, but not their Spanish. Then a Tejano friend from El Paso came up and asked what I was working on.

"My Spanish paper."

"You want help?"

I looked at him. "You speak Spanish?"

"Dude, you've heard me."

"I mean not like orale wey vato loco. School Spanish."

He told me his uncle was a lawyer in Juarez and he used to work in his office.

"Well, thanks, man."

He helped me make it better. I passed Spanish and had the requirements to graduate college. Done with the help of two Chicanos who called me Scott.

11.

Ramona Diary of SRD: Interview with Joaquin Murrieta Number Two

The rest stop was right by an orchard so tourists were filling up their trunks with all the reachable oranges as if they had never seen oranges before. Other than the picking and trunk packing, and some orange hurling food fights of a few kids, the historic rest stop was empty. The copper plaque detailing Ramona's journey across the state was worn and unreadable save for a light squiggle moving through what must be California with a faint star that must be where I stood. Nowhere.

Since this is America, though, nowhere can be a tourist trap of Spanish California as well.

I was tired, yet I needed to talk to the head Joaquin. There was a painted fiberglass old west horse tie up in front of the bathrooms, by the parking lot. Someone lying down in their car looked up when I lashed the mule I stole from the Joaquins to it.

"Hey amigo! Amigo! When my husband comes out of the bathroom can we have a picture?"

I felt awkward talking to someone when I had a human head in a bag. "No sorry, no."

"You look so authentic. A real desperado."

I thought about saying you wanna see authentic and showing her Joaquin's head but instead I said, "I'm busy! Leave me alone, lady."

"But we came all the way from Chicago."

I escaped into the men's room holding Joaquin in a saddle bag and shut the door. Moldy wallpaper had the whole novel of *Ramona* printed on it, though you'd need a ladder to read it all. The entire length of time I've had him, since the escape from the bandit palace to here, days ago, the Head Joaquin hasn't stopped babbling, but I was afraid of a bandit posse chasing after me and bringing me to bandit justice or injustice for stealing what's left of their leader to stop and listen to him. On the shelf above the sink, Joaquin kept up babbling in his jar. I knew I had to pull him out. Touch his whisky pickled dead flesh and decades of unwashed hair. He looked at me through the amber liquid and shouted, looking like a dead bandido fish. I reached in past the freely-floating-in-whisky hair to the too-matted-or-welded-to-the-skin hair underneath. I gripped, retching. I pulled him out. He smelled like pig's feet and pickle juice.

I set him down. He dripped and oozed. He had longish hair and a droopy mustache that was wet and slick against his lips. Century old three-day stubble covered his orange-gray cheeks. I threw up in the sink, no surprise.

He glanced down at me and said, "You're no bed of roses, yourself, güero."

I had to breathe which meant to breathe his stink in once more, which made me throw up again. I asked him, "Do you know anything about Ramona?"

He was quiet. Dripping. Dead eyes rolled over in my direction. Then he talked.

I won't write down his lies, his inauthentic claims, or the cover-ups he used in responding to even to this simple question, which lead me to believe, whether through age or the dire trauma of beheading and preserving, or the torment and anguish of dealing with his century long disability, that Joaquin had forgotten who he was exactly.

After my tiring line of questions, I asked him point blank if he was Felipe Moreno, and he said indifferently, "I dunno, güero." I said, "If you are, we could be related." He grunted, "Go and get your cousin here laid then, cabrón."

I wanted someone who could link me to the past and help me find the jewels, and what better than a Chicano folk hero to help in that. But Joaquin was just a head. The head of a jackass who didn't remember anything. Here I decided not to tell him about grandpa. Not so loving Grandpa Love.

I was no further in finding the jewels of Ramona, in regaining my lost inheritance than when I dug up Helen Hunt Jackson. I thought of the weeks I've lost looking into dead ends, the (empty) life I left in Texas. I wanted to grab Joaquin and smash his head against the mirror. Then I thought the restroom was angry, too, because the walls began shaking.

Joaquin shouted, "El Diablo está furioso!" His head quivered on the ledge, flecks of pickled flesh and whiskey sauce hitting the mirror. One of these flecks hit my mouth and I spent a few seconds spitting in what I believed to be my first earthquake since I got back to California. Then I realized the noise and shaking were too localized for an earthquake, and rather came from one of the doors of the restroom stalls.

Thinking a pipe had shaken loose from its clamps, I kicked the door open to end the noise. There, in front of me, was a tourist, pants down next to a plastic grocery bag filled with oranges from outside. Orange pulp was mashed on his chest and the dead soldiers of used oranges lay about his feet. In his hand he held a fresh orange wrapped around his vitamin C enriched phallus. He was hunched over and reading a chapter of *Ramona* on the wall, lost in the story. For half a moment, I inadvertently wondered which chapter that was and he turned to me and it seemed as if he were going to offer me an orange to join in, but then El Turista saw the dripping Head Joaquin on the shelf. He yelped and dropped his rind-lover. I quickly stuck Joaquin back in the jar. El Turista, half naked with pulp and love spread all over him, got out of the men's room quickly.

Outside there was a ruckus from the lady who wanted a photo who must have been upset with her husband running around pantless with an orange dick. I crept by their yelling. At least they didn't want a picture anymore and let me escape with two heads: Joaquin's and my own. As I led the mule away, I decided two things. To name the mule Helen and to take Joaquin to Grandpa Love, the ranger who caught him. The man who cut off his head. Joaquin will be good for something after all.

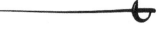

12.

True Son of Ramonaland: Who's Who in Ramona

A nice primer to quiz the kids and to shore up those faulty memories of ours! Ready pard?

Ramona

Heroine. A Mexican half-White and half-Indian.

Alessandro

Mission Indian whose sheering skill and singing makes him palatable to the Spanish ranchers. He absconds with Ramona once he learns of her secret Indian heritage. Eventual atheist.

Felipe Moreno

The effeminate Spanish lord of the ranch, step-brother and future husband to Ramona. He fails at being American and flees to Mexico.

Don Moreno

Hero and general of the Mexican-American war who owned Rancho Moreno, which lands in dire straits due to his death and the loss of his guidance.

Dona Moreno

Canny and cunning Spanish widow. America hater. Ramona hater.

Old Juan Can

Californio proletarian who oversteps his bounds.

Helen Hunt Jackson

The exalted bard who traveled Southern California and sung her epic out on to the page and into our hearts and the land. A tourist of Southern California herself!

Aunt Ri

Fun-loving simple rustic who befriends and aids Ramona and her Indian husband.

Joaquin Murrieta

This ill-renowned bandit has been shoe-horned into Ramona's story by many hack authors of serials and dime-novel rags. His death and those of the bandits of his ilk assured the dominance of Americanism in our beloved land.

Captain Harry Love

The first California Ranger. The man who brought justice to the outlaw Joaquin Murrieta. The white man who made Ramonaland safe for you and me.

Zorro

Zorro is not officially a part of the story, but as a legendary *Californio*, the first words out of a tourist's mouth after, "Where is Ramona?" is "Where is Zorro?" And so Zorro is depicted on many billboards and posters, dancing a fandango with beautiful Ramona. In how many movies has Zorro saved our queen? How many church bells has she been urged to jump off of? How many times has she landed in the arms of Zorro to be whisked away on the back of his black stallion, Tornado, to secluded groves appropriate for love? We Ramona pilgrims must calm our learned objections to this mating of the 18th and 19th centuries. As in the many movies where a De la Vega passed the tradition of Zorro, this "True son of Ramonaland" has also adopted the Zorro appellation, though not a gallant leapers of belfries, but humble author of this guidebook and an expert collector and amateur anthropologist on all things Californio.

13.

The Ramona Diary of SRD: The Car

Everyone who lived where we did had a nice car, a successful businessman's car, like dad. People who lived in town or the reservation between our house and town had old, shitty cars or trucks with dents, rust, or Bondo on the sides. After school, my sister and I would melt in the crowd of kids at the pickup spot as we worried and wondered if it would be dad or mom that would pick us up that day. Cadillacs with bright chrome in the high desert sun or one of the new mom minivans, always dark blue or burgundy, would pick up our neighbors who'd wave bye to us, but there were always kids left and one friend who wouldn't go away. Eventually, a once-white car, crying and sweating rust from all edges, rumpled from many dents, ceiling lining falling in stringy tears like a mad woman's unkempt hair, rattled, groaned and sputtered as it pulled in. It wasn't just what people thought of a poor person's car, it was a dirty person's, a crazy person's car. A white trash car, but from the driver's Brown skin and black hair it seemed the car of a destitute reservation Indian. A broke, crazy beaner car. My sister and I had white names and were silent on who we were most of the time, as if the other kids couldn't tell. The car was our Brown sides crashing into the curb, cussing and yelling you fucking kids get in from over here, I can't get this friggin' car started again. It was our mom's car and it was our angry, slovenly mother screaming. The neatly dressed, fair-skinned friend that wouldn't go away asked us if that was our maid and I felt our skin on fire as my sister said who she was. In front of all the delighted kids from town, we stepped away from the upper middle-class white space we pretended could be ours because of our house and father's name and got in the car. We clicked our seat belts in the poor and Brown, the native, the subjugated, the mentally ill, the desperate, the space that, even in our native land of California, would always drive up to us unannounced and always be the crazed, cursing face of our mother, yelling get in the car, you don't belong.

14.

True Son of Ramonaland: Meet Captain Harry Love

Background:

In the wild days of the Gold Rush, just after the Mexican-American War, California wasn't as safe for you or me as it is today. That safety we all enjoy and in which we prosper is owed to one man alone, Captain Harry Love, the first California Ranger.

Things to do:

For a pittance you can shake hands and have your photo taken with the man who made California safe for every American. Listen closely! He is unbelievably old and is a living relic from a bygone era where justice danced from the barrels of white men's guns and from the ropes of the posse. Relive the wild days of Ramona and view the cracked daguerreotype of the lady of California shaking hands with the hero of California. Touch he who has touched Ramona. Daily retellings from the man himself start at 2 pm.

Zorro's Note:

A great place to leave the kids, if they can fend for themselves for a while. With no electricity or running water, children will make do with tales about bringing law to the lawless land, hunting and fishing anecdotes, and what makes a good dog.

15.

Ramona Diary of SRD: Grandpa Love

I worked it out once. He's really a great grandpa, but I forgot how many, exactly. He's still grandpa.

I could see his tip jar still had the same starter two dollars signed by some president for luck.

"Grandpa?" I had to remind him, but eventually he remembered and shouted, "There's my boy!" Grandpa Love hasn't had all his marbles in a long time. That's what Dad told me, even when I was little. That used to confuse me since Grandpa had two jars full of marbles—ancient ones with dust settled and caked between.

Grandpa kept a lot of things in jars, especially the head of things. The cupboard looked like an Aztec skull rack, with the dead eyes of dogs he really loved, raccoons he really hated, and a thug or two looking out of the bog-mire of whiskey in the jars. He talked to them. He talks to everything.

The meaner the people in our family are, the older they can get. Grandpa isn't as mean as his brother, who demands to be wheeled to the park so he can throw rocks at Black and Chinese children.

He shook my hand. Grandpa doesn't hug now that I'm grown. I sat. The shack stunk like I knew it would.

The jar with Joaquin Murrieta's head was in my backpack. Head Joaquin was spinning, angry. He knew Grandpa Love's voice. I could feel the vibrations from his cussing in my back.

"I got you something Grandpa."

Grandpa normally gives me a couple of guns or a squirrel's tail each visit. It's nice to have something for him for once. I set the jar on the table and pushed it up close for him to see.

"Hot dog! Murrieta, you dirty greaser, you can never get gone for long can ya? Love will always get you, heh-heh. Love conquers all, ha, ha."

Grandpa hugged me. My Mexican grandpa didn't talk much but showed his love by being strict, teaching you right from wrong, and he worked hard though he wanted you to read books and be smart. Grandpa Love didn't really teach anything but hunting, but I saw him get by through swindling, deal making, violence, and threats—in other words he took me on business trips with him. He also had lots of dogs and had taught them all to steal. In each cage was a type of stealing dog. Candy-stealing dog. Breakfast-stealing dog. Dog-stealing dog. And always his favorite, whiskey-stealing dog. As a kid I used to ride some of these dogs, so you could say I was an accomplice when I rode them out and they came back with me on top and a box of licorice in their mouths.

I thought about all the redneck ways he taught me: how to hunt critters, how to trap critters, how to make things out of nothing, how to find useful trash and save it and never use it, how to believe you can fix anything, how to love dogs. He told me all about Mexicans and what he did and how the state would have been without him. He always almost treated me like family though he normally said I must get lots of sun.

"Bandidos will just be damn bandidos, nothing strong in 'em. No voice in 'em like Murrieta. That's why he's in that thar whiskey, to shut him up. I cut the fucker's head off and he wouldn't shut up. All the way from the valley to San Francisco he wouldn't shut up in that sack, damn near had a dozen Messykins chasing me, wanting a revolution. That Murrieta is no hero, he's a killer, kill a White man or a Chinamen as soon as spit."

"Jo bar boo!" Joaquin said and banged in his jar.

Grandpa went on and on about the future, about building a theme park. He said he was going to put this and that over by the shack, and people will stop here again. People would be wary of the wetbacks coming in their back door and remember who the hell he was, what he did and why he did it. Joaquin hopped in his jar, head hitting the lid. I didn't say anything, I just stood. "Finally get rid of the last greaser. Clear the land."

I was angry with Joaquin not guiding me to Ramona's jewels. I didn't want to leave him to what grandpa was saying, which made me think Joaquin and I could find the jewels together. And that since I had taken his head from the other Joaquins, we indeed have become partners. I put the gumdrop jar in front of Grandpa and took up Joaquin's. Love talked on, getting confused and lost in his vision of remaking his shack into Dead Mexican Disneyland.

Joaquin quit jar hopping as he saw what I was doing. For the fourth time, Joaquin Murrieta's head was stolen. From his body by Grandpa, from the circus by bandits, from the bandits by me, and now from Grandpa by me. All the thieving dogs in their kennel were wagging tails and barking, happy that I finally learned something from them. As I tied Head Joaquin to the mule, he shouted the old Californio battle cry, and I understood him in his murk for the first time.

"¡Viva California! Abajo Americanos!"

16.

True Son of Ramonaland: Ancient Sources of *Ramona*

Has there always been a Ramona story? The bard of California, Helen Hunt Jackson, tells us she engendered the Old West epic purely from stories of fallen houses and hanging Indians in her travels of Southern California and her own imagination fused with the wonders she saw, smelled, and heard. Nonetheless, many an amateur scholar has stumbled across many an ancient record that supposedly proves to be the true ancient source of Ramona and colors Helen Hunt Jackson a hack plagiarist. Rather than sully this revered matron of letters and enter the nonsensical fray, your guide to all things Ramona, Zorro, offers this informative list as further proof only that *Ramona* indeed is a timeless story, lived, and repeated throughout the ages.

Your humble guide will end this query by saying everything—even everyone—has a precedent, even Californio queens and indignation of the barbarian and irk of the grasping civilized man as they come together.

We must remember HHJ repeatedly swore that she based the love of Ramona and Alessandro solely on a trashy drawing of Dante and Beatrice, of which she had a copy. We must admit Romance novel covers themselves serve as a precedent to *Ramona,* as well as these connections made by the deluded.

1. The single line in *Medea* where the titular character moans how she looked forward to marrying her half Greek sons to a Greek princess worthy of their standing despite her and their Asiatic origins. Perhaps these little butchered hybrids were spared further pain after all as we see how Ramona suffered due to her 'Asiatic' heritage.

2.A surviving letter fragment detailing a Roman father, a former frontier soldier in Germania, informs that his daughter has run off with a trusted manservant, one Esoteric, and admonishes other Roman citizens that true Roman blood and upbringing cannot undo the wilds in any admixture with these supposedly docile savages.

3.A Norman girl testifies in a legal document against her supposed Anglo-Saxon blood. She states, "I don't have an ounce of peasant savage in me." She also says she'd sooner marry a sheep than a long haired mustachioed English sheepherder.

4.A "lost" Icelandic saga that details a Viking woman who burns her brother in his sleep for killing her Skraling lover. She absconds the destroyed settlement with the family jewel horde of a hundred Viking raids.

5.Additionally, some quack scholars have made much of Cortez's own half Indian son (and the whole of hybrid Mexico) El Mestizo, Martin Cortez, of being the inspiration for *Ramona*. They use Martin's quest along with his White brother in gaining the inheritance of Mexico, much like the Spaniard Felipe, searching the land for the half Indian Ramona, to take her back into her ancestral estates of California.

6.Another potential source is drawn from the 18th century family bible of Elizabeth Lemonseedtreeton. Her wavy, near illegible and semi-literate script has been translated by some as a letter, which accompanied the bible to a prisoner convicted of some unknown crime who also seems to have been her adopted daughter.

"You were a little dark baby we saved from the ashes. Your daddy must have been one of these French trappers that lurk about. If not for your blue eyes we would have burned you with the rest of them. You were our little Brown acorn. It broke my heart you turned to black magic and sexed my natural son.

I hope this here book learns you the true Christian way and that savage blood in you dies like the rest of those devils in the village." Other scholars, however, contend that it is merely a mnemonic technique for baked goods recipes containing acorns and, "kitchen magic for lean times."

7.How many drooling proto-scholar has shut down offices with their letters of proof or burdened internet forums with the so-called link to Toypurina, the rebel? Indeed she was the sorceress with green eyes who threatened the Padres and Corporal Verdugo and declared those mentioned must die for their intrusions upon Indian land. And wasn't this Indian queen captured and sent to live on a ranch with a new Spanish husband much as Felipe captured Ramona and once again uplifted her to ranch life, but now as ranch matron? Again, much like half Indian Ramona, Toypurina has been an inspiration for insipid romances in hack novels.

17.

True Son of Ramonaland: Café Ramona

Background:

Once a simple diner called Joe's, when Café Ramona's owners obtained Baba and Capitán in a card game they transformed the greasy spoon into the fine dining establishment of today. The mission style façade and the busty waitresses in colonial skirts all bring to mind the Old West. A simple, lazy era where one might digest food at ease.

Things to Do:

Relax and indulge yourself in *Californio* cuisine. One may stroke the still luxuriant fur of Capitán. Careful! He was not only Ramona's loyal dog, but also Colonel Moreno's, who fought so bravely against the American juggernaut. Always keep in mind his upbringing as a Mexican dog of war. Testament to this are the scraps of the pale blue trousers of a US soldier still caught on his daggerish teeth.

Zorro's Note:

Despite numerous requests, horse and dog are not on the menu.

18.

Ramona Diary of SRD: Mexican Hating Dog

Café Ramona is a truck stop and no one should eat here. The menus have border bandits and leggy dancing girls on them and the Mexican food comes out of a box you can see in the kitchen that says auténtico. Ramona's horse is easy enough to find—Baba hangs in the middle of the greasy spoon and a chalkboard with the soup of the day nailed to him. On top of Baba, a rag doll sits in a Spanish costume and has a stitched smile.

A stuffed horse doesn't help my appetite, but I make the grave mistake of eating anyway. On the inevitable run to the men's room, I find Capitán, Ramona's dog. Though he's stuffed, he's meant to scare you: huge, shaggy, teeth bared, glass eyes missing. He did startle me and it made me remember once I moved past a dumb, deaf, and blind dog just like this. Jay, my best friend in junior high, had a dog like Capitán, but his was a Mexican Hating Dog.

I'd been over Jay's place lots, but I had never been to the barn where the dog was kept. Jay told me all about the Mexican Hating Dog, saying, "He might hate you, or half hate you." I just pushed him and said I'd kill his dog if he ever let it loose. The dog's real name was Rose, though it was a boy.

The day I met the Mexican Hating Dog was when Jay's dad picked us up from the mall, an hour away, and down the mountain. His dad was drunk, and I was embarrassed and scared all the way up since he turned the wheel with his whole body, all the way to the left and all the way to the right with each curve. When we got to their house, I was happy to be alive, happy to hide from him in Jay's room, but Mr. Newman said we had to feed the horse and the dog before we got to play Nintendo.

Jay was pissed that I saw his dad drunk. After we fed the horse he said he was going to let the beaner-eating dog loose. I told him I wasn't going in then, that he should feed the stupid dog himself. He said, "It'll be alright, the dog's blind," and he got a bucket of dog food from the shed.

The Mexican Hating Dog made me wonder, though. Was I Mexican enough for him to hate? And how does the Mexican Hating Dog tell a White boy from a Chicano? Could he sense something Aztec or could he just smell cumin and jalapeños? I was taller than most Mexicans and Jay was as short as most, and I thought that this might throw the Mexican Hating Dog off, but then I remembered the dog was blind so height wouldn't matter. Jay's dad thought I was Italian or I wouldn't be allowed over, so the fact that they had a Mexican Hating Dog didn't surprise me.

I, scared of the Mexi-test, helped Jay carry the feed bucket as he told me how Rose bit illegal after illegal—Pedro, Hugo, Hector—all the guys he had to work with in the yard. "Hey, you like Hector," I said. "Rose didn't like him. He got stuck in the cage and Rosie bit his ass." "Hugo wasn't Mexican, he was from El Salvador," I told him, but by then, we were outside the giant dog cage.

Massive, shaggy, and white, the Mexican Hating Dog stood slowly and came towards the gate. "Hey Rosie, I got you another beaner." "I'll kill your dog for real, dude." The gate was open and I set the dog bowl down. I tried to be nice—this was still just a dog. "Hey Rosie, want some food?" The glossy-eyed dog snorted mucus and huffed through his maw. The Mexican Hating Dog growled and snapped at me.

Jay closed the gate quickly. "Bite his ass Rosie, bite his ass." "I'll kill your fucking dog, man!" Jay opened the gate and I pushed through. He told me, "You must be Mexican enough not to like."

In Café Ramona, I noticed half of Capitán's teeth were gone. The real Capitán or not, I guess this dog bit his share of White boys before ending up stuffed in a truck stop.

There wasn't any space on the mule for a stuffed dog, much less the horse. I unhooked Capitán's collar—thick leather and brass. As I climbed on the mule outside, Head Joaquin said I should wear it for luck. The circle of brass only said "Capitán" and the collar fit around my neck on the last hole. "How do I look?" He said, "Shit, I was joking," and as we rode off once again he said I really looked like a pervert now.

19.

True Son of Ramonaland: Ramona at the Movies

Our exalted Spanish Californian heroine's tale has not been limited to the printed word of Helen Hunt Jackson's *Ramona, a story*. The tale of Ramona has been taken up not only by pulp and quasi literary hacks, but also by genius film directors of the age. Here, to provide complete Ramonan information, is a list of Ramona films and their summaries.

Feature films

1. Ramona

A silent tour de force detailing the fall of Spanish California to the American juggernaut.

2. Ramona

Black and white 1934 shot for shot talkie remake of the 1915 silent classic.

3. Ramona

Colorized version of the 1934 remake of the silent 1915 classic loosely based on the best-selling novel.

4. Ramona 1980

Ramona is a sassy SoCal girl in a controlling Latin gang. She must make a choice, between her love of a White cop and a Latino gangster, and also a priest who wants to leave the collar for her. Ramona is armed and dangerous and in your neighborhood.

5. Dance with Ramona

A wounded American settler recuperates on the Moreno Ranch and falls in love with the half-breed Ramona and her bucolic, feudal culture dedicated to dance and song. The settler comes to realize that Californios and their simple ways must be preserved, so he takes the fight to the American thieves to protect everything he believes is his.

Art house films

1. Marrying Alessandro, Marrying Gaia

Ramona, a White college girl, falls in love with the Indian Alessandro and his pro-Earth culture, only to fall out of love when she learns Alessandro is just another long-haired Mexican gardener.

Foreign Films

1. Le Mexicain

A beautiful French spy named Ramona infiltrates the Moreno Ranch. Can she fulfill her mission to blow up the ranch, or will she become enamored with the dashing Spaniard Felipe, his people, and the sheep?

2. Chica de Estados Unidos

Mexican version of the Ramona tale.

3. Ramona: Brotherly Love

A Korean film about a Mexican ranch girl who cannot deny her lust for her brother, who plots to overthrow the US government. During the siege of Rancho Moreno, Ramona and Felipe give themselves to concupiscent incest before they dance their last fandango of bullets.

Ramona Horror Movies

1. Noche De Los Californios Vivientes

At night, the American who bought the Moreno Ranch for a quarter of the price can't sleep. He hears the sounds of fandango dances and loud "Ah-ha!s" in the wind. He gathers his family, who hears nothing, and barricades himself in one room just as a horde of Mexicans assault the ranch. He blasts Hispanic head after Hispanic head and lops off many groping Brown arms. He shoots his own son when he says papi instead of pops. The room gets overrun and his wife and daughter are dragged away while the rancher lunges for the cellar. As he dies, he hears the fandango resume with his wife singing and his son and daughter dancing.

2. *Raging Ramona*

In 2045 all humans have died, leaving only Mexicans. A girl named Ramona wakes up from an underground stasis capsule and finds she has been infected with the Chee-Kahn-noh virus. As her skin darkens, her hair blackens, and her eyes glow Brown, she must not only find a cure, but find a way to survive in this hot and spicy nightmare world.

Ramona Pornographic Films

The back-alley fleshpots of Hollywood have had their way with Ramona as well. The titles of these films are included for completion only, and the plots are left to the reader's learned imagination.

1. *Sheep Shearing Time*
2. *No pants Nepantla*
3. *Dirty Mexican Dancing*
4. *The Squatter and The Don*
5. *Rancheria Debaucheria*
6. *Half-breeds Have Needs*
7. *Ramona, Two Worlds, Two Dongs.*
8. *Mexican-American Whore in the Mexican-American War*
9. *Ramona Kissed Here…And Here!*
10. *Flip her, Felipe*

20.

The Ramona Diary of SRD: Wrath of Mom

The one time I can remember my mother doing something pleasant for me that didn't include beratement or martyrdom was when, on a whim, she took me to the theater in the early 80s to see *Star Trek II: The Wrath of Khan.*

I didn't even know the movie was out, but I watched the TV show every chance I got and, because of the best yard sale ever, had nearly all the huge 8" Star Trek dolls—Kirk, Bones, Spock, Scotty, and Sulu. The only ones missing were Uhura and Chekov. At the theater, when I saw that the uniforms were not like the primary colors on the TV show or the pastels of the first movie, but Brit Red Coat red, I felt disappointed. The villain played by Mr. Roarke was scary, powerful, and I wondered if Khan was a Mexican name. Montalbán was famous for playing the Latin Lover stereotype: he danced and overpowered women in tropical resorts in all his movies. And Latin Lover is what the role of Khan called for in the original episode "Space Seed" where a female officer betrays the ship for his over-passionate jerky manipulation. With the Latin Lover typecasting and the Mexican actor and his accent in mind, *Wrath of Khan* can be seen through a Chicano lens…or rather through how the White consciousness views the "Chicano problem" in the terms of the Cold War empire. I can hear everyone saying, "Nah, no, way," and "How is this related to having one nice time with your Mom?" Think this word in Ricardo's voice: "Patience, my friend." And remember how Khan is a genetically engineered "superhuman?" An expression of the threat of Mexican so-called hyper-masculinity and the "eugenics" of raza cósmica. Remember Khan's "banishment" after a defeat and the manner in which he says, "On earth, two hundred years ago, I was a prince...." How more Chicano can you get! Every Chicano, even me, says we were lords of the land, all that ranchero stuff that puts Spanish words all over city names and street signs. And of course, the wrathful over-passionate Khan. Passion, the Mexican stereotype's downfall. Mix in the latent Anglo fear of a "vengeful Mexican" poised to strike and win Aztlán back, or at least the family ranch that's now subdivisions for yuppies. Chicanos, the monsters that lurk in your backyard while you worry about the enemy on the other side of the world.

It can be said the one nice time I remember with my mother was seeing this movie where we were the villains, the scary monsters. My mother, after all, gives me my connection to being Chicano and the "The Chicano Problem" of being the male monster, the bandido, the gang-banger, in Anglos' nightmares.

Some of this was a bit in my head when I watched the show. I mean I was only a kid, but I knew that Puerto Rican on the cop show "CHiPs" and that it was about heroes or big villains who vaguely looked like me in the mainstream. Even the White guy playing Zorro the Gay Blade (which, despite its problems, is awesome) didn't look like me at all and he was supposed to be the Ur Californio, my own Mexican ancestors. I'm not like Miklo the half-breed from *Blood In, Blood Out*, my skin doesn't take after my White father other than the curse of the Scottish ruddiness.

Unlike the rest of the family, Mom didn't even like science fiction or action movies, so I wouldn't expect her to watch anything of the sort with me, especially as she called all my boyhood TV shows and cartoons fucking stupid as she did me. My Dad and sister were off somewhere for the evening. We were about to go home where I expected a night of hiding from her insults and screams in my room and playing with toys to distance my fear of her coming in and rampaging my books, favorite toys, or me. Out of nowhere she asked, "Do you want to see that Star Track show, Scotty?" "What Star Trek show?" And then we were sitting with the slow space whale battles of Khan's vengeance and the Enterprise looming over us huge. And like George Costanza says, it's a hell of a thing when Spock dies. It was also a hell of a thing when charred-ass Khan dies. When his boyfriend says you have proved yourself superior: we have a starship we can go anywhere, do anything, Khan won't give up on revenge, "He tasks me and I will have him!" All that Mexicans never forgive stuff. A more fitting Chicano ending would be Khan saying, "No shit, ese, I'm not wasting laser power on that devious güero. I'm taking my raza cósmica gente and finding a chilo planet para fumar mota." It's Kirk's and the screen writer's bad conscience—the master's unease about the state of the empire.

And the movie is about fear of our indigenous ties. Khan calls those little mind-eating ear bugs the "last indigenous" creatures, which we are. Mom's and Khan's unhappiness with being blocked from power. Mom taking it out on a proto-emblem of patriarchy in her charge, unfortunately for me of both Anglo and Latino power structures. Khan looked to lead the sellout colonized agents by reminding them (or chew-minding via the ear bugs) of their indigenous ties, their otherness, and Mom wanted to punish me out of resentment. What did she have against me? A boy in her care she could let out her demons on for how men treated her? Who knows.

I loved her before the age of five. She was a nice mother, did things for me, and talked to me sweetly. For whatever reason, after five, she began shouting, acting crazy, and taking everything out on me. Calling me fucking stupid, as if it were my nickname. Breaking my toys or ripping my comics and throwing them at me when Dad wasn't around and calling me a goddamn liar when he came home from his business trips. I had always felt there was a family in my immediate family of four, but I wasn't a part of it, even more so when my father moved out. Mom's insane yelling, smashing, and insulting became so normalized when I was a teenager that I stopped trying to avoid it, because there was no avoiding it. Me and Mom seeing this movie with a Chicano view of it...maybe she was nice because the movie was already showing what the Chicano male is in the American imagination: a monster. My future then as a boy. Perhaps I make too big of a deal of it, but it's odd that this is the only good memory I can think of her. She did things for me as other Moms did in keeping up with Jones' manner, but those "nice" things and activities always came with belittling, souring my memory of them. Why did she hate me? Take things out on me? I don't know. Because she could.

After years of not speaking with her, I tried to reconcile due to the urging of my Dad's brother Billy Bob (yes, his real name, as I always have to say. I am half Texas redneck) who didn't want to hear my side and only considered my mother an eccentric. I tried. Told her when we were alone, that though we had a bad relationship, we could be mother and son from now on. She lay on her bed, windows open letting the cold San Diego night in and blowing her black hair around. She didn't even look at me. She said, "Oh I don't care." Then, "You think you're so fucking smart." That took me aback, of course. I told her she was a crazy person, and from then on, I didn't have a mother and walked out. The next morning, with my sister there, she made us breakfast, which she never did in seventeen years of having lived with her, and tried to act like a White 1950s TV Mom, as if fried eggs (which I hate) could make up for it being too late for reconciliation.

Kirk the great Anglo hero is an asshole living in fear of those conquered and colonized. Of those he has marginalized. And half-breeds like me are always suspect. His best bud has to die to prove himself a good house Vulcan, for his half-breed ass to finally be considered "human" or centered in this Anglo-centric space fantasy. I don't know what I could have done to make my mother act less crazy toward me. Probably only what I did, banishment to Dad and Texas, certainly the dark corners of the universe in the arrogant imagination of most Californians.

Mom and I watched all the movie, the drone of passing ships buzzed our seats via the giant speakers, and the sound of exploding ships crashed in our ears. The great White hero felt young again. We left, and Mom said it was okay, a bit silly, but okay. Then I hoped as I did many times that this would be the start of a nicer, less wrathful mother. Us doing things together other than her yelling at me, breaking my stuff, and embarrassing me with her temper and weird bag lady mien that caused my White friends to call her "The Squaw" instead of "Your mother" or "Mrs. Duncan." Yet even at seven, I knew the nice time wouldn't last. Whatever my mother had against me she never let it go and I was always subject to her wrath. And now as a man I know why she was nice that one time watching that one movie. Those who own society, no matter how much I read, accomplish, or speak like them, see me as a monster, something to be distrusted and conquered. And so Khan's wrath and Mom's wrath was to be my own.

21.
Ramona Diary of SRD: Zorro y Joaquín y Yo

Zorro. Zorro the wannabe Californio. Zorro the copycat. The Joaquin Murrieta knockoff. Zorro from the comics is paternalistic to the Native Californians, just as Zorro the amateur anthropologist is paternalistic to the quaint so-called "Spaniards" of California. The amateur's book, *True Son of Ramonaland,* is in my hands now, and his self-declared name ZORRO is in caps on the cover and "Zorro" himself in a black cape and mask with that straight brimmed hat. His book that started falling apart as soon as I started writing in it for a diary.

Zorro had to know more than he put in his book about the jewels of Ramona, fictional heroine of Spanish California. Though my companion, the head of Joaquin Murrieta, wanted a violent comeuppance and insisted we kidnap him, so we could, "Tomar nuestro tiempo." I kept telling Joaquin that the Zorro we were going to see isn't the one he is thinking about. He's not the guy who wrote that story in 1917 or whenever, capitalizing on the fantasy around Spanish California. Here I swore to never mention Batman to Joaquin as I have enough on my plate with Ramona and Zorro. I said instead, "This Zorro is just another White nerd who wrote a book."

The empty bus rattled from the bumpy road and our argument caused the eyes of the bus driver to lock on me from her mirror.

"All Zorros are rip offs of Joaquin! He will pay the price of the other's folly!"

"We just can't jump Zorro, the cops would be on us like white on rice or Whites on Mexicans."

"You are no Joaquin! A Joaquin does what he needs to for justice.

You are now just some pinche sidekick. Cut off your fingers like the last guy."

I'm leaving out the rest of the argument we had about who is the sidekick that continued though I stuffed him back down into the bag that I carry him, his head, in. We stepped off the bus where pedestrians must have taken me for just another crazy screaming at himself, but we both got quiet in front of Zorro's movie theater.

We jumped the little pay stall and pushed the big old wood doors to the theater. No attendant to be seen. The lobby held display cases filled with pots, baskets, fencing swords, distressed santos with paint peeling off their wood posed in awkward positions, bultos, statues meant to be walked around, and retablos of even more painted saints on the walls. Zorro's much vaunted collection is filled with objects and expensive price tags, but empty of humanity. The only noise came from theater number one, from behind the carved painted door with an ancient Spanish couple locked in some kind of fandango dance.

In theater one, written on the screen were the words CALIFORNIOS! Zorro, chubby, short, in costume was presenting to a group of kids. The theater was ornate, with Victorian faux Greek columns, and murals of Indigenous people working with missions in the background and caballeros riding in finery. I only noticed those things later, because though I wanted to be calm, civil even, I recalled every bitten page of *True Son of Ramonaland* and what he had said that made me bite it, and Zorro became the center of a fuzzy red room of a thousand screams.

He looked up at me. I must have looked like Brown Charles Manson. Traveling for a week with the Joaquins, traveling for another week running from the Joaquins, and traveling for yet one more week with Head Joaquin alone had left no time for me to attend to my toilet. My hair had grease and twigs. My eyes had that sleepless burning. My coat caged some smells, but how much stink slipped through, I didn't know. With each of my steps Zorro Can I help you sir-ed me, the shelter is the other block-ed me, this is a private showing for children-ed me, we don't have no trabajo here-ed me till I was close and he just screamed, "Oh God, oh God," and shoved little children in between me and him.

My tongue fumbled over anger and my natural mumbling. I let out a row of nonsense that must have sounded like Martian beeps and growls.

Joaquin banged about in my bag. "What the hell is that shit?" Then he said we're here for a chingasos, a word I now feel comfortable to write as it has been a couple of weeks since the gang of Joaquins had handed one out to me.

Zorro didn't understand my proto-language and just said, "Don't... Don't hurt these children, or you will suffer the wrath of Zorro!" And he put a protective chubby paw on a kid's shoulder, who sneered up at him.

Then it all got ugly and way out of control. But it was the kids. Little White children have lost all sense, don't I know having grown up aside them. They're raised in an entitled world without discipline. It was more like that *Island of Mr. Bureau*, animals in human form, than that "Nuts to your asmar" from that other book, *The King Flies*, I think. The kids tore into Zorro. They could smell his fear, and children hate fear. And so they gave him the Anglitos chingasitos.

Zorro's big belly quivered on the floor, "Make them stop, make them stop." I just stood there, enjoying this minor comeuppance. Joaquin yelled so much that he wanted to see, I brought him out so he could and held him over little heads and the dolorous beat down. Zorro went from shielding his face to clutching it, saying, "Dear sweet Jesus…" or something like that as whisky dripped off Joaquin's face and he viewed his rival. The kids yelped, "Wow! Cool!" And the fifteen or so little stomping legs stopped.

Joaquin spoke. Made demands, rather. "Reparations!" "Movie rights!" And he kept calling him, "Pinche payaso!"

Zorro just started crying, "What do you want, don't hurt me." All that kind of boring stuff.

And the kids kept saying, "Wow!" wanting to touch Joaquin's zombie flesh.

"What I want is for you to tell me about these Californio antiques."

"They're, they're just replicas."

"Then tell me about Ramona jewels!"

"The jewels?"

"My grandma told me all about them. We're Californios."

"Ha ha!" his hands dropped. "You peasants believe in those? They aren't real"

I stepped closer as I was about to start punching his rude, lying mouth. But the kids mistook it for me, shoving Joaquin in his face.

"Yeah, make 'em kiss!"

Joaquin started shouting, "Hell no, I didn't sign up to kiss no White boy!"

But I did it anyway. "You love Californios so much? Give Joaquin a kiss!"

Zorro's chubby balloon face went pale and Joaquin's seemed to turn from gray to green. Then Joaquin the Real Deal and Zorro the No Deal kissed. Or better to say they twisted in my grip as I held them mouth to mouth.

All the kids—"Ewwwwww...."

Then Zorro went damn crazy and started tonguing Joaquin so hard I had to pull back his head and put him down. But I should've known. Being face to face with real Californios is too much for most White people, much less for Zorro with his peculiar hobby made real, live and in 3D in his own theater.

Zorro started chanting, "Yes, the jewels! The jewels!" He clutched me and just before I knocked him in the head a few times with my diary, he said, "Your folk spun family oral tradition must mean they are real. The jewels, the jewels, children."

Then Zorro waddled up the aisle warp speed and was out the old timey movie doors. Joaquin cried and said he was glad his mother was gone now that he was a homosexual and I had better steal something to make it worthwhile. I said, "Don't be a homophobe," and all the kids looked at me expectantly asking, "What's a homophobe," and I said just a kind of jerk. Joaquin whined, "No one made you kiss no fat gabacho!"

Whether Zorro called the cops or not I didn't feel right leaving the apocalypse children to their own grubby devices so I got them to help out in the lobby looking for the "Ramona" artifacts and to get them to stop calling each other homophobe. We opened all the display cases and busted the lock to the storage room. Zorro wasn't lying. All replicas. And all for sale. Made in China hidden under every pottery lip, hiding at the bottom of every hilt. I let the kids have what they wanted, as I imagined the children who made them in a sweatshop in Asia didn't get to play with them. La policía would bust me in a moment anyway. Zorro had dropped his mask in the aisle. Something for me so I could have something from this other than a bad taste and probably more arguments with Joaquin. Then moms and dads came back and saw their wee darling armed with replica hats, swords, and pots. Terrible little turistas dressed as Californios and me, the mad half Mexican Manson presiding over them.

"Have fun kids?"

"Yeah!"

"Say goodbye to Zorro, everyone"

"Bye, Zorro!"

My crest fell so hard it broke on the dirty floor with the popcorn: They couldn't even tell the difference between me and Zorro. Had they been drinking? Or was it bad parenting? I mean, why would they leave their kids in the care of a freak like Zorro? Perhaps there is enough fake-ass Zorro in this half-breed for it not to matter.

I followed everyone out, no posse, no policía. On the sidewalk, one little demon child, the one who bit Zorro's leg till bloody and who now held a replica Californio coffee cup, looked up at me. "Mister, I really liked your head." Of course he wanted a human head, he probably wanted a whole rack of them.

I put my finger to my lips, shushing. Though I didn't hit Zorro other than the few back and forward slaps across the face with my diary, I still felt I had done something wrong, other than thievery of cups and hats, and inciting a riot amongst juveniles. My heart was sloshing around in taquera sauce. Now Zorro the fake, the wannabe, the Made in China ersatz, would be looking for Ramona's jewels, my ancestor's jewels, my Californio inheritance for real.

22.
Ramona Diary of SRD: Captain Beaner

Each night, we set up camp. It's cheaper than a motel and we get to see more of the land this way. Head Joaquin said it brings back old times for him. "What about you, Capitán?" I didn't say anything. Since I wore the dog collar, he's been calling me that instead of güero for a few days. Being called Capitán brought back old times for me, too. But back then I wasn't Capitán. I was Captain Beaner.

There were lots of neighborhood kids. We ran wild over Ramona, up the hills of her flanks, down the breast valleys and up and out her nose running from bat caves and coyote dens.

Our neighbors weren't only coyotes. Migrant workers (though everyone called them illegal aliens), just boys too, farm boys from northern Mexico camped in the hills and mountains around our neighborhood. My dad (who spoke the best Spanish, or at least would admit to understanding what was being said) came home every few weeks and on the weekends would hire these guys to work in our yard. Most everyone had big yards and animals and horses and bullshit projects their fathers gave them, so weekends were not free time from school, but usually hard labor. We'd move the same hill of sand back and forth between the front yard and the corral while my father decided what to do with it. We dug trenches for sprinklers and of course, chopped and chopped bushes of various alien species I was allergic to.

The guys would ask me if that was my father in Spanish. I would say, "Sí." They asked if I wanted to take a break. I would say, "Sí." When my dad showed up again we both would attack the ground, chop, chop, pretending not to see him, and then stop as soon as he left.

All my friends and I worked alongside these boys, who slept out at night or, if lucky, were allowed to stay with someone or had a collective house to stay. When we were older, we would ask them to buy beer for us and so if we didn't know a few of them we certainly used their services in more than one regard.

We were running around the hills when my friends and I came across a camp in one of the few shaded places. No one was there. My neighbor Chris said, "Cool, beaner camp." Chris kicked things over while Jay emptied sacks. There were other guys throwing plaid shirts up trees.

I said, "Hey, we might know these guys," and tried to push Chris off a pack of clothes. Chris pushed me back and said, "Look, he is defending his people. Captain fucking Beaner. Defender of his gente."

Yeah, Captain Beaner. Hero of illegals.

I was ashamed and stopped. What could I do against so many anyway? And they, sons of corporate vice presidents, tore up some poor people's few belongings. This was the only time in all our vandal fun I had thought we had done something bad.

Then the smashing of bottles, ripping of clothes, and pocketing of coins stopped. Their commotion over a magazine drew me away from my anger to come back. I looked over everyone's shoulder and saw angry blue-eyed Ramona, chest bare. On the page pirate shirts and skirts lay heaped on the ground next to ads for Spanish phone sex. Pale Felipe and long-haired Alessandro stood next to her, their dongs in her hands.

"Wow," Jay said, ripping the page off for himself.

"Beaner bitch mag."

23.

Ramona Diary of SRD: Don't Be So Sensitive

Grandpa Fernandez is New Mexican, not in the "I moved to New Mexico because it's like so spiritual man," hippy way, but nuevomexicano. Our family were colonials and locals and stayed in New Mexico for nearly four hundred years till grandpa moved to LA to be with grandma after the big war. Like most New Mexicans, hispanos, Grandpa always said he was Spanish or like I've heard other New Mexicans say, "I'm Spanish! I'm only a little Zuni, Apache, Pueblo, and Comanche!" Granted we must be some Spanish, but I'm always leery of such insistence. Though our family seems to get our Native looks from grandma's Californio side more (or Soboba, colonized Natives), I wouldn't discount Grandpa Fernandez having a lot more color in his hatch chilies than just the few Mexica I found hiding in our family tree.

On one of grandma's and grandpa's visits to our house in the San Diego Country Estates, the all-White upper middle class area between Ramona the town and the Barona Indian reservation, I was showing grandpa the other way to get to the main road by walking a bit and showing him the turn. He didn't say anything and I at twelve years old was afraid of him, especially since this was before he chilled out in his later years. We crossed back towards the house and some young White guys slowed down in their truck and shouted, "GO THE FUCK BACK TO MEXICO YOU BEANERS!!!" Grandpa ignored them but looked mad. I didn't say anything at first, glad they didn't stop and also seeing how mad grandpa was, but then I said, "Sorry Grandpa, not everyone is like that around here," though most of the

White people were. And grandpa gritted out, “Those guys are jerks!” I felt ashamed, but I was also used to hearing, “Fuck you, Beaner,” and the occasional bottle or piss jug aimed at me from Anglos as I walked down the roads of the Country Estates or even in town by myself.

Walking back to the house with grandpa, I knew better than to say, “Think we are so Spanish now?” which would have gotten me a slap for disrespect. Yet I was tired of the Brown experience, something that drew in all the danger and suspicion in my life from other kids, teachers, cops, clerks at the mall, security guards, and the parents of friends who wouldn’t let me or any other Mexican in their house. And I wanted to protect my grandfather, a man who fought fascists abroad for the fascists at home, from all the fuck you beaner’s I heard nearly every day.

We got back to the house and everyone, my family, was around the pool, being loud, eating and joking, my sister and cousin swimming. Grandma telling a loud story, slipping to Spanglish. I felt as if something was wrong with us. Being native here, Indigenous people, New Mexican, or Californio…it didn’t matter: we’re just dirty beaners to everyone. I wanted to club the jerks in the truck and bury them in the desert. All that redneck respect for elders never applies to old Black or Mexican men.

I told dad what the guys had yelled at me and grandpa. My White father probably couldn’t imagine how bad it makes you feel, worried every passing mullet head driving a Ford truck in the country might pop out and bash you. People tell me to fight one Mexican, fight the whole enchilada, but I’ve had to run from the whole Anglo casserole many, many times.

I wish Grandpa Fernandez had talked to me about the jerks in the truck. The thing my White father couldn’t tell me, despite the advantages of him giving me enough White blood and a White name to confuse society, was how to survive as a male minority in America, something I had to learn for myself battling the whole casserole my entire life. Grandpa could have told me something, like what he did when he couldn’t buy a house or land because the owners told him they don’t sell to Mexicans. Or what he did after he yelled, “I didn’t fight in the war for this!” when the cops murdered a boy my age in his front yard and my aunt was pulling on his arm and screaming, “Daddy they’ll kill you!” as the police circled him.

In the dining room, wrapping up food for the fridge, probably enchiladas and casseroles, I told Dad I didn't like what the jerks said, especially to grandpa. He said, "I know." I said, "I hate living here." Here being not our house in the Estates with a pool, but the entire Southwest, my own homeland. I talked to him, but I knew he didn't know and didn't want to understand the danger, the fear, or the constant treatment as a monster I would face every day. All he said was, "Don't be so sensitive."

24.
True Son of Ramonaland: Jewels Clues

Here Zorro adds a few well-known clues to find Ramona's jewels as well as others gleaned by intensive investigation by our authors. Just remember to share some of that loot with me!

*Whatever artifact, antique, witness, etc. you find, be sure to shake and look at both sides, and turn inside out.

*While the enthusiasm of amateurs for California history and gemstones is appreciated, pot hunting is disapproved of. If you suspect you have found a treasure, please inform a learned, accredited scholar, such as the author of this guide, Zorro. Our history is precious and the objects that hold testimony to it should not be trodden upon or ridden roughshod or smashed to bits even if they don't possess material value. If it has to do with Ramona, someone loves it.

*If you do not find anything authentic pertaining to Spanish California, please go to the website found on the back cover of *True Son of Ramonaland* and peruse Zorro's own personal collection to fulfill your need with offers of replica Spanish California objects d' Ramona. Get a real headdress like Alessandro or a bandit mask like Zorro!

Well known clues

*No record exists of Felipe Moreno or Ramona owning a strong box in any LA area bank.

*Though there are many fakes, there are no descendants of any Morenos in Mexico that have inherited any wealth as described in *Ramona, a story*.

Zorro's gleanings

*The so-called 'Ramona's daughter' claimant turned out to be yet another in a long line of frauds only interested in the wealth of Ramona lovers. The quest is not over, the jewels may lie at the bottom of the cereal box as it were, and if we shake California, we can hear the jewels are there.

*Old timers from those long past days of Ramona, many of which reside in California, tend to have no valuable information. Think, if they knew where Ramona hid her jewels all this time, wouldn't they have collected them in their distant youth? This doesn't prevent them from taking advantage of the rare attention and spinning an ancient sleep-inducing tale that has no bearing in the world.

25.
Ramona Diary of SRD: Stuff I've Found

Ramona's Colonial Dress

I asked Joaquin how in the hell does having a dress lead you to a treasure horde?

"Recreate the world, cabrón. Don't you read penny dreadfuls? The hero finds a glove and then he knows who the killer is. Shits got monograms."

I told him monograms won't help. But I turned the dress inside out, made some tears in the lining (which I sewed back up later) and a small glass vial spilled out, inside of which was rolled a note. Though vindicated, Joaquin said nothing. I carefully unrolled the paper which was as long and half as wide as my palm. In a hellishly small micro-script, a rather long story rode the length of the paper. Yet, it was in Spanish. I could understand historia, arboles, lobo, gigante, dientes, rojo, abuela, but nothing else.

Joaquin was angry at my lack of faith in his logic and wouldn't translate. "Learn Spanish, pinche güero." We glared at each other through the whisky haze of his jar until he grunted and began, "Ah! Bay! Say! Day!"

The pistola of Señor Moreno.

I know guns a bit, though I deplore them. That said, the pistola of Señor Moreno's, Ramona's step dad, was begging to be shot. Joaquin loved that we were strapped now. "It's a tool. Tarjeta de crédito!"

"How do you know about those? Robbing ATMs?"

"Yes, smartypants. Los Joaquines brought one to the cave. They thought it was a slot machine. It didn't work, you need those little cards, tarjetas de créditos."

"If this pistola is a tool, why am I fixing all this gold wire on it?"

"If some pendejos see you with a rusted up pistola, you are just a thug. You got to have style, medio güero. My sidekick needs to have some flash himself. Why do you think I got gold dust floating in my jar? I look like I'm in a discotheque. People need to have an exciting experience when they meet you."

Joaquin looked like a corpse in a milky jar filled with river water, but I didn't spoil his self-image.

However, I did look good. The silver thread really shined and I looked like some kind of rotten black-hearted movie villain with the pistol thrust in my belt and the powder sack jangling on my side. You don't see so many Brown heroes portrayed, so a fancy villain had to do.

"Hey, how will this help us find Ramona's jewels?"

"What kind of bandido are you? If you want to get your family jewels back, you need a gun."

Grandma's handkerchief.

A faint tag reads (maybe) "Hecho en China."

No help.

Capitán's collar

Been wearing it, spike and leather. A little scary, but if the gun was meant to add flash, a leather collar should mean business. Or I'm a mutant freak, which may be the same thing. On the other side of the tag from where it says Capitán it says:

"Mi casa es Rancho Moreno."

Joaquin made me mad by saying, "That ain't no clue." I shouted you're the one who suggested grabbing antiques left and right.

In the silence that followed our argument, I flipped the tag to make those little clinky noises against the buckle. I thought about tourists ravaging Rancho Moreno. Anything not bolted torn off for souvenirs. Other than pulling off the boards for yokels back home has anyone really looked there? Who would leave an inheritance of jewels and move? Did they really move? Who knows better than me that Californios didn't go anywhere and are still kicking.

26.
True Son of Ramonaland: Majella Trail

Background

While many of the springs and shade trees that gave Ramona (dubbed Majella by her barbaric husband, Alessandro) respite during her long journey away from Rancho Moreno, they are not extant now. Sadly, the rush to create Majella themed convenience stops for the traveler used what little water was available and the desert reclaimed the land.

While the trail is littered with many ghost-malls, these half-built husks, while a lure to the amateur frontier photographer, should not be entered as the wind, or even the sound of your hoots and hurrahs as you pose, could bring what's left of the roof down upon you.

An even more important warning than falling debris from the abandoned structures of the Majella Trail is that of the danger of the Californian Griffin (*Gryphus Californicus).*

Zorro's Note:

The Californian Griffin

Every boy in California knows that the deserts are filled with dangers to any would-be Tom Sawyer. The worst of the beasts that threaten the adventurer is the famous Californian griffin. Imagine the surprise of Conquering Cortez as he named our fabulous land after the fictional Amazon queen Califia from the book *The Adventures of Esplandian* (an obvious tourist ploy) to find real griffins. While Califia proved to be a ridiculous Spanish myth and her crown of California long passed to our beloved Ramona, the California griffin is a very real cousin of the indigenous cougar. Unlike cougars who prey upon small women or young children, the griffin preys solely upon males of any species. While a hiker upon the Majella Trail may fear wandering into a desert meth lab, their carcass is unerringly found with the telltale claw and beak markings characteristic of *Gryphus Californicus.*

This danger has been scoffed at as the west coast jackalope, and it is due to unscrupulous types with backgrounds in taxidermy creating a cat-bird amalgam and swearing they caught the beast and selling the trophy to inexperienced drooling bumpkins. Don't be fooled by such hucksters into thinking the griffin a fable. THEY ARE REAL AND THEY EAT MEN.

Ramona, a story glaringly omits this danger of the California trail—griffins. The author who reported Ramona's amazing life story, Helen Hunt Jackson, stayed with many welcoming *Californio* ranchers. They surely wouldn't have allowed their honored guest to traverse such dangerous areas, and dutifully neglected to mention this horror so the great east coast lady could sleep peacefully without night terrors of what may hover just outside her window.

Survivors and spotters of this danger have described the *Gryphus Californicus* as, "large as a New World lion." The descriptions of the avian features of the beast have ranged from a radiant eagle to a death raven with the same menacing call. It is best for the traveler to be wary of any bird of prey, lest it prove to be a man-eating griffin.

27.

Ramona Diary of SRD: Aztlandorado

Joaquin and I were lost in the middle of nowhere and found a wooden rickety shack to at least have one point of reference. The shack could be the shack Alessandro and Ramona built and that Aunt 'Ri the rustic claimed, but whether it was or not became of no importance. What was described in *Ramona* as forested has now been turned to desert by the deforestation and destruction for barren parking lots and abandoned shells of houses no one wants. The door didn't seem strong enough to block a bear and the entire shack seemed like it might come down if one or two coyotes or a mountain lion willed it. Wild creatures have surely returned even if they were once scared off by the noise of the pile drivers decades ago. Dorothy didn't chant in her "Oh my" line about flying monkeys. Likewise, griffins were not amongst my worries.

Outside to relieve myself, I saw griffins circling us in the air. I turned and saw several growling and blocking the shack door. Claws and beaks clenched my back. Joaquin, sitting on the middle of the shack's floor, had no hope. There was yelling—he must have been spinning in his jar as the sound oscillated between loud and soft. From the corner of my eye a gray griffin swooped past me from the shack, carrying Joaquin's head away.

I worried for my friend and felt, perhaps, my story was at an end, because Joaquin was my guide, the one who knew the world before it was broken up into the pieces I was born in, though he didn't seem to remember a damn thing. A swipe scratched my face and tore my glasses. I lashed out where I heard squawks with my home defense machete.

I fought in a myopic fog, moving by the sound and tactile feel of the pecks, scratches, and the brush of feathers. Anger overcame fear, yet later I wondered if there was something else that could have done other than fighting, lashing out with my own claws as it were. The griffins were animals and the fight made me one: organs and feathers squashed in my grips. A puddle of human and griffin blood and downy feathers formed underneath me. In this crazed myopic time where I slashed with hate and paid no mind where bodies lie, I'm somewhat positive that blood and bits of bird-cat meat landed in my mouth. A grotesque taste of the rechewed remains of what lay at the bottom of a fried chicken bucket of which there is no forgetting even if someone believes it's acceptable to eat your enemies, human or animal. I swung more and more in the air, then heard the warbles and chirps in a distant circle from me. The griffins had backed off, but why?

At first, I thought it was because it was dawn. Golden light spread everywhere. Gold in the night. I scrunch my eyes to see down the gloomy trail. Women in gold. Some with gold teeth and noses. Their skin itself seemed to prefer gold tinge or covered in gold dust and oil. The women didn't speak to me. The griffins transformed from beasts into subservient animals—pets rubbing chins on the women's strong calves. The women walked, with no words spoken. I followed, too hungry, too lost without my glasses, too tired for questions and followed their smell as much as followed by my weakened sight. The smell of Amazons is electric, intoxicating.

Soon I was then in a city of Amazons with gold facades of pyramidal temples shining with moon light and the murmurs and press of many curious and muscular women, as I found with my myopic palming of arms and bellies along the path I was shoved along. The rest of that night, I bathed in a golden tub. Their queen, Califia, welcomed me the next day.

My myopia and poor sense of direction won't give many clues, but I will try to not add any as they could lead to demise. The Amazons are not only dangerous, they don't wish to join the world outside the Majella trail. Much of what I saw must be left to the imagination and opening to the possibility that I, dehydrated, hungry, desperate, lonely and bespectacled, might be wrong. What I thought must be gold could be dried mud, majestic temples could be old sci-fi backdrops to billboards from the '50s. Yet, I may have glimpsed what the lost place Fray Marcos must have seen—houses of gold, stairs of gold, warrioresses and what Montalvo wrote about Califia. El Dorado and Aztlán. Aztlandorado. I have been where many have died to find.

Later the next night after the fight, I sat petting an orange griffin as it purred and chirped. I gained one's trust enough to lift her wings and inspect where feather meets fur and even pet her downy belly. They are living vivisections. The Californian griffin is actually the size of a house cat. That body of a lion stuff is hype that makes survivors sound manly. Griffins don't have eagle heads, either. More like the heads of vultures. The cat parts are nearly all tabby. The orange griffin had the usual stripes of an orange cat, and its feathers were dark red. A Persian white griffin had extraordinarily shaggy feathers and a golden beak. Griffins like this may account for all the pioneer sightings of angels lifting lost, starving settlers into good riddance.

Was this a cat or a bird? She purred. When she was tired of that she sang. The feline added warmer mammalian aspects to the avian, and, of course, the bird allowed the cat to fly. From our battle I saw the strange flight of the griffin—the tail acts as balance and accounts for their sharp maneuvers and hard turns. Like most fights where nothing is lost other than a few feathers and a little scratched out blood, we were friends afterwards.

I slept most of the next day. Joaquin was brought to me in a basket. He was pecked and had many gashes. I sprinkled whisky from my pack over him and sewed mangled cheeks back together, his head transforming from that of a zombie to that of a Frankenstein. The thread the Amazons had given me was gold, so now Joaquin had yellow zigzags holding him together.

I didn't wonder why the head of Joaquin didn't cause them concern as their streets and halls were filled with the decayed heads and toothless skulls of men. It brought to my mind the Mexica's tzompantli, the skulls racks of honored victims. These women seem to respect the taking of trophies and made me think of the beheading of Joaquin and the bodies of other Chicanos and Natives that Americans put on display of our defeat. Perhaps the fact I held Head Joaquin's head is why they allowed me to live, and eventually, to leave. I, an Indigenous Californian, gringoized or not, had taken back a trophy of defeat.

In the morning, two especially large Amazons with golden faces led me to Queen Califia by hand motions. No one—me or Amazons, or surprisingly Joaquin— could understand the other's language, and no one seemed intent on learning. The rest of my meeting with the queen is private.

Unlike the skeletons in cuirasses and dead be-overalled miners, I knew the gold, real or mud, wasn't mine. Amazons admire its beauty but don't covet it. Greed and bad examples were changing me. I began to feel a claim on the place, the mud/gold, the blurry bodies of women, and began renaming things as had one of what many believe to be the first bad example. My myopia only allowed me to see bits of people, and to keep them apart, I called them things like Big Breast Plate, Gams, Round Ears, Soft arms and while I could blame my myopia and what my weak eyes land on, differencing people on what parts you see isn't nice. This is perhaps why no men are here and I had to leave. Why was I allowed in and then forced to leave? While I had proved myself by retaking Joaquin's head, in the city of the Amazon, I failed the test of gold, of Amazons themselves.

The next day I was led away. How I wanted to stay with beautiful Califia. The memory agitates me now, and I hope again to get lost enough to wander into their city. There is no going back. Satan never returns to sit with God in heaven, Odysseus never swims back to Ogygia to sleep with Calypso. When I left, Califia tenderly gripped my shirt and drew me up to her and kissed me. (She is an Amazon queen, after all, at least six five, or maybe it was the gold-plated heels). She then put in my hands another enclosed basket. Beautiful gleaming women with spears then jabbed me till I was out of the Amazon city, and they tossed my glasses in a desert lime green bush, which took me an hour to find. By then of course, the Amazons were gone. Farther down the trail, heading towards places on the map, I lifted the top of the basket Califia gave me. Cradled in dry grass and feather down, was a griffin egg.

28.

Ramona Diary of SRD: First Night in Texas

Dad picked me up from the Dallas airport. The golden age was about to happen compared to my former life. Dad's world was laid back, logical, where rules had reasons. It was late at night and in the car he told me I was staying with Uncle Billy Bob for now. I was mad, asking why, and then, why didn't you tell me, neither of which got an answer. I loved my uncle, but his house wasn't home.

I hadn't thought things through when I yelled back at mom. I didn't have much choice, though. I couldn't think of any friends that would have let me stay with them. I would have tried squatting in the semi-wilderness, hiding my homeless status so I could go to school and be near my sister still (I knew some kids who had done this), but I thought life with dad would open doors more fabulous and be a permanent emancipation from my mother.

Later, dad and I did live in an apartment, but not for very long. It was only North Dallas, but seemed very urban to my small town eyes and I had little points of reference on what to do. Uncle Billy Bob and Aunt Sonya came over and took me places on the weekend since Dad often left me alone to be with his girlfriend. So much that eventually I just moved in with my aunt and uncle permanently. I had a new, Whiter family.

Though in the apartment by myself I would learn to replace the lonely complaints of coyotes with the exasperation of trains, that first night in my uncle's house, newly arrived from California, the trains kept me up. I stared at strange walls feeling like a poor relation, a problem handed off. Yet, I didn't think it would be a long time before I moved back to California. It was home.

29. Ramona Diary of SRD: Pickles the Warrior

Most Mexicans don't like cats. Grandma was one who did, as well as my mother and one aunt. Grandma had a black cat with a malformed stub for a tail and of course got called Stubby. After grandma organized my aunt, cousin, and sister into clean brigades each summer day, she and I would sit on the bed and she told me stories as she folded clothes or read *The Enquirer* pulled from one of her towers and towers of stacked collections. Stubby would strut in and hop up on the bed. There was an onyx jaguar statue, a stretching cat with an open maw, on the headboard and I'd ask Stubby if that was him. Obviously, my sister and everyone was always upset at me for listening to stories, learning to sew, and playing with stubby instead of cleaning. I was the littlest and the only boy.

My uncle, grandpa, and every other Mexican seems to hate cats. They don't work. They don't seem appreciative. They cause allergies. They are picky eaters. If you are thinking that sounds a bit like you, you'd know how I felt as a kid. I loved dogs, birds, rats, every creature, but I thought the cats I knew were some of the best people around. I didn't like to hear them maligned. Especially Pickles, "The mean goddamn ass cat you guys have," like my not-cat-liking aunt said.

We got Pickles when I was little, three years old, the age when everything happened. I think she was meant to be more of a present to my sister as I was blocked from the view of the kitty and she was presented to my sister and asked what to name it though they said it was for "both of you guys" which by then I knew really didn't include me, but it was a kitten.

I hoping to see the new tabby kitten, heart of my heart, furry eater of tenderloins or Friskies. What do you guys want to name her mom and dad? asked Clara. Porky Pig! I shouted, as Porky Pig talked just like me and I liked his cartoons. No Scotty. What did you say, Clara? Pickles.

I tried calling her Porky Pig after that anyway, but Pickles was Pickles.

Pickles was Persian and tabby. I knew she was a battle cat because when she was almost or hardly a year old I heard Clara screaming. Mom mom! There's a snake. Goddammit what are you fucking kids screaming about now (ok, my mom didn't talk to us like that quite yet. After I was 5 she called us shits and goddamn kids and bastards. I can't really remember her being nice, these nice years because of the punch-drunk mist of abuse, so we have to have the foul-mouthed creature who in this instance, this era, would have been nicer).

No goddamnit, it's a stick, you called me over here for fucking nothing. Slap (slaps like this came later as I said, but I can't really remember any other way).

No mom, look at it. By then I crept over and looked. Ah! It's a snake! You fucking Scotty, you're a goddam boy, go pick it up and take it out.

(So if you knew me for two seconds as a mother should have and you'd see I was not the kind of kid that liked picking up gross mysterious creatures and getting dirty.) I said, Nuh uh.

Goddammit get a broom. Mom hid her face and cringed. In this overblown domestic chaos, curious Pickles strutting right through the alley of it.

She stopped and peered at the green snake. Not missing a beat mom said good get it Pickles! Pickles sauntered over and batted it. Kill it, kill it! Pickles laid down and batted it more. Out came the crazy lady "no!" so much like too much LSD hippies, the mentally ill scream I'd hear from her the rest of her days. Don't play with it!

I remembered there were grass snakes and there wasn't a rattle, like I saw in West Texas. (I was an experienced three year old). I got the scooper Clara got the broom and after it seemed Pickles had killed it, Clara pushed it up making ick noises and I ran with the demonic cargo in my hands. I flung it. Clara was petting the purring warrior and Mom said, good cat, good cat. I pet the warrior cat too and asked if we should have a funeral for the snake. What are you fucking kidding? Pickles went off to the back to look for her defeated enemy.

Pickles survived other things. Boys hired to clean the yard threw her in the pool as I ran up against them and then got a towel. Pickles put up with getting dressed in doll clothes and pushed in the stroller as the neighbor lady asked to see our baby and I said it was a cat and she screamed, scaring the hell out of Pickles and she ran out shaking her legs in her booties and bonnet. Pickles killed every day in Plano, Texas, dragging squirrels back for me and my sister.

Pickles was the only cat we had that could outsmart coyotes. She killed an array of desert creatures. She put dogs in their place with one swipe.

Pickles was the warrior cat who slept every night at my feet, covering them with her Persian tabby fur. My wild majestic maned defender. The savage queen who brought me rodents and warmed my feet. Cruel to everyone else, she for some reason, perhaps something like the warmth of dying patients that lures sleepy hospital cats, chose me.

30.

The Ramona Diary of SRD: Captain Kirk Wasn't a Doll Like That

This was '79, maybe. I was four or five. I was young, I know that, but old enough to know certain things weren't done. It would have been different if I had wanted to, but that wasn't the case. Mom had just put my sister Clara's baby doll in my hands and said, "Play with this."

We were at my grandparents' in LA and it was too scary for me to play in the front yard, but my aunt and cousin Rebecca lived next door. At the end of the long driveway was a tiny convenience store where shady kids hung out. Grandma would grab my hand if I waved to them, and told me in Spanish they were street trash. The shady kids looked high, or as I thought in my too young mind to really know what high was, all sweaty. In between the houses, there was a square of yard hidden from the road, the only place I could play on my own.

I sat there in the shade from the roof where there was dirt and a spot for me. When we got ready for the trip back to visit California, Mom said I could bring one toy, and it was between Luke Skywalker and Captain Kirk, but Luke sucked without his X-wing, which I didn't have so it was Captain Kirk, the toy that I fixed the balding painted swirl of plastic hair with Brown felt pen all the time. I also hand washed and inspected his uniform. I thought he might have been real and didn't want him to show up and see me with an unkempt plastic version of himself.

Mom put my sister's baby doll in my hands. I said I didn't want to play with it and got a slap. Mom went back to her baby talk. "I want you to be sensitive." I was mad. I knew my sister would be mad too if she caught me with her stuff, the one toy she could bring to play with all summer. I had no interest in baby dolls and it was an insult to Captain Kirk to have him replaced by a baby, even a giant mutant one in relation to his size. I put the doll on the side and said I'd play with it later and Mom pulled my ear. "Play with the goddamn doll now," she gritted. My ear hurt and I didn't want another slap, so I said okay. She left smiling, all high minded, having done some misguided hippy feminist duty by slapping me. I considered how one plays with a baby doll. I had seen my sister do so, but it seemed boring. I bounced the doll up and down in case mom was looking and wondered how long I had to play with it and how long I could keep pretending to play with it. All of a sudden, the doll disappeared and I got knocked hard on the head.

"Fucking f_____! What the hell are you doing?"

"Mom made me, Grandpa!"

Grandpa never said anything and when he did it was either funny or scary. This was scary. I really hoped mom was about to get some of that head knocking when she showed up and he asked her why she would make me play with a doll. She whined that she wanted me to grow up to be sensitive. Grandpa muttered, "Aw, fuck," and threw the doll against the wall. Mom cried and went away. I stared at my sister's doll, wondering if I still had to play with it. It was really quiet and I didn't move, didn't touch anything and then Grandpa and Grandma were talking loud in Spanish and mom started talking louder in English, then it sounded like, the only time ever, she started yelling in Spanish, but it was far and behind a wall, so maybe not. I couldn't run to Grandma, which I normally did. I looked at Captain Kirk with his ready for all adversity knitted brow. I grabbed him and went in through the other side of the house, where the chili peppers were hung. I slinked to a corner in the living room by the couch where my aunt was reading Grandma's inquirers. She had her lips pressed together in a half smile. "You okay m'ijo?" I said nothing and wished I was on another planet or the Enterprise. My sister was about to slam open the front door and yell, "What did you do to my doll," and my cousin Rebecca would call me a sissy for the rest of the summer and tell her friends that played Marco Polo with us that I wanted to be a girl. But, before any of that, my aunt twisted on the couch and looked over at me.

"You know, Scotty, your Captain Spock is a doll, too."

31.
True Son of Ramonaland: El Camino Real

El Camino Real! The dream! The pastoral interlude. How the image, the very words, El Camino Real, King's Road, has become interchangeable with the notion of Spanish California, and even the dream of all that is Ramona.

Here on this road, this modern Ramona Highway, gallant caballeros, centaurs of California, rode rancho to rancho, trading one worn horse for a fresh one at each. They defended each other from banditry and Indian revolts, calling each other hijos del país, native sons. Every Mission and accompanying presidio, or fort, a day's ride between on El Camino Real sinewing up from San Diego de Alcala to far northern Yerba Buena.

And to this day still, it seems due to traffic jams, it remains a day's travel between every Mission, every Ramona Attraction, for the beleaguered tourist.

Do not be tempted to stop your station wagon, sports car, or electric monstrosity and just get out on El Camino Real's asphalt or give up on your journey and form tribal alliances with those fellow tourists in similar modeled automobiles. You will get there, your place of interest, your Real Ramona eventually.

Yet, do, as you sit in hot cars, windows down, fumes of hundreds of engines worrying your cancer anxiety, daydream and allow the Spanish Colonial style that colors every rooftop with accompanying tropical palms lull you to linger on those Spanish tiles shaped on shapely Indian maidens' legs as we all know and your day dream to bring you back to that sensual age sans fumes and traffic jams or screaming, bored children, and when the only concern was hospitality and the barbeque, dancing, music, the celebrated fandango hospitality entails. Conjure up the flashing eyes of señoritas, all welcoming to the American traveler, the tourist, or the tales of the old folk to lull you further to the even older days, which regaled Helen Hunt Jackson, when the Dons of the ranchos reigned supreme. El Camino Real, the one of old and the paved one of now will take you there....Wake up! Cars behind you are honking, pard. You will get to where you are going and find your own pastoral tale, your own Ramona, just as Helen Hunt Jackson did. Your own Spanish pastoral to enjoy before modern American reality calls, honking again....

32.
Ramona Diary of SRD: Fan. Dang. Oh...

As a kid mom taught me and my sister to dance to shake shake shake your booty disco. While I was pretty good and looked 1970s awesome with my flowery polyester shirts with butterfly collars, we didn't keep it up. As teenagers my sister was supposed to teach me to dance, but I got kicked out and the family broke apart before that happened. I never truly learned anything beyond awkward swaying. Yet, people, women especially, always expect me to dance well. And get extremely disappointed if anything more than a close dance is required.

I'm saying all this because as my thoughts were on the Ramona Play, wondering if my Soboba great grandfather ever saw it, I wandered into one of those ethnic dance shows. The kind is always out of its original context and that has more to do with sideshows than dance routines. And this dance wasn't some dance only done deep in the Congo of Mexico, dragged back and meant to delight the Victorian Anglo tourists. This was a fandango, one of the dances Californios are famous for and that appear ad nauseum in all the Ramona movies. The reverse of my hopes for the play.

Other than happy pastoral entertainment depicted in the movies, fandangos were also the ruin of my family and most Californios who threw one too many fancy parties. Expected to dance away their land when the US was too eager to deprive them of it. Ramona dance movies as well as indulging in exoticism, mock the "Fall of the Dons." The US had to invade, we Mexicans were dancing! And, as always, we Californios are falling in everyone's imagination.

On the tarp that was supposed to be a stage everyone was standing around, there were young women spinning in big silly dresses. At the edge of the dance circle tired, I looked at the girls as their dresses whipped up high. Then it became my turn to feel the creepy gaze of strange eyes on me. A fleshy man in a tight blue Hawaiian shirt, bolo tie, and a giant novelty sombrero ala Cinco de Mayo was taking my picture. The geriatrics next to him saw and all began to hold their phones towards me, lean back due to farsightedness and tap the screen to capture me forever.

After the patching and repairing and cleaning of my clothes by the Amazons, I have a nineteenth century look with my Californio hat and though my clothes are a bit worn the gold threads give my outfit a glitzy look. Maybe that's why the Cinco de bolo Hawaiian shirt guy started taking my picture. Maybe that's why, all of a sudden, I was pushed out with the dancers under the sonic umbrella of the screeching singer and seated guitarists. Dancers twirled beside me… they stunk! The reused costumes were heavy with sweat and the brownish dust of makeup to cover light skin so they may better fit the role of a "Spaniard."

They pushed me. "Who are you?" they hissed. I tried to find a hole in the square of pressed together tourists and wound up by the singer, who seemed perturbed and eyed me. Attractive, dressed as every sweaty night dream of Ramona ever, dark Spanish dress, pale neck, dark eyes, herself heated in mist on a hot day. She said, "It appears we have a guest singer," and hung the microphone in front of me, offhanded yet insistent. I was about to say, "Please let me out of here," but she was lovely, insistent, and I despised the tourist eyes upon me, so I had a rare dramatic moment: I swept my left arm with the gilded sleeve, fanny pack tourists flashed for their pictures, I heard someone say he looks just like that Ricky Ricardo, and I remembered how handsome I think I am sometimes, and what a romantic figure I must seem from the outside, with my boots with broken gold spurs, my sombrero with the flashing cat toys, and Joaquin's bandolier and the Wonder Woman-looking gilded lariat. I took a deep breath, looking as if the most entertaining song ever was about to leap out from my chest and into the air and said, "This beaner won't sing or dance for you."

33.
Ramona Diary of SRD: No Mexicans Inside

When my friends and I played cowboys and Indians, I had to be the Indian every time. The cowboys always murdered us and killed our so-called squaws, who always had to be there, awaiting death at the inevitable failure of our raid. I wanted to play a cowboy or just win for once and kill some frontier wives, but my friends always said no. I asked why, they said I looked Indian, wasn't I an Indian? I had to be the Indian. And the Indians were the losers, so we always had to lose.

I knew I was a cowboy too, my White great uncles showed me the early Anglo-Texan handwritten account of our great great whatever father's life of murdering Indians, squatting on their land, and murdering Mexicans at the battle of San Jacinto. My White father looked like my friends' fathers, but their grandparents were always from Germany, from Italy, from Poland, from Ireland. So, I knew I came from not just Indios and vaqueros, but cowboys as well, and way more than they did. They were Whiter, they got to be the cowboys. And the cowboys were always defending their fort, their homestead, their space, and somehow we Indians were both the invaders and those that had to die.

Cowboys would shout, "I'm raping your squaw and cutting her head off!" I had many squaws to rape and behead for cowboys, that was what they were for. "I have your entire frontier family and I'm stabbing them and they are screaming!" "—No, no reset. That's not fair. Real Indians are supposed to die."

My mother's family is "real-ish" Native American "from LA." We were from LA forever it seemed. Though everyone said we were of the "whothefuckarewe tribe." Mission Indian from my grandma, at least one Mexica ancestor and probably Pueblo and Apache from grandpa's side. We are the mixed leftovers from the earlier conquests of Spain and Mexico. Dad was some Comanche but was so White it was like the Southern White and Black myth about having a Cherokee princess in their line to make it seem they had a connection to the land and a legacy, never mind part of the Southern White legacy is the atrocities committed against Cherokees. For Southern Blacks, not having to own up to having White slaver blood (who could blame them) and having a "free savage people" fantasy heritage. Both White and Black people were always telling me "I'm probably more Indian than you!" as if being colonized was a prize.

My father's side's chant of our heritage Scottish, Irish, Comanche, ended with "Black Dutch." No one knew what the hell that was, maybe like Black Irish. I found out it's an Indian trying to pass for White. As a kid I looked at Quanah Parker the half White half Indian maybe great great grandfather like a close family member on my White side since I saw he might be more like me than the rest of the Duncans who often talked about the "problem with wetbacks and coloreds."

Most Indians I knew dressed like cowboys. Including our hispano relatives who mostly were ranchers. Cowboys won the war, including the fashion war. Everyone else I saw in Texas and in rural California were ropers, urban cowboys. Rednecks who dressed and fantasized about the genocidal frontier life of being an "outlaw."

The only other Mexican kid in the neighborhood David would be able to start out a cowboy as he was better liked…and fit the Mexican phenotype of short and stocky better. Midway through he'd get pushed over to my side as there weren't enough Indians. If other kids from down the block joined in, whatever White kid had fallen from grace would be pushed to be an Indian and look at me and David with disgust and then tell us his grandmother had Cherokee blood and high cheekbones. He was a "real Indian" and "not a dirty Mexican." I normally said, "We will call you chief White-ass Dennis the Menace then."

Most of these White kids that had to join the Indian side I'd have to fight. They took their anger on being a loser on the loser side out on me, but I was a big kid for my age. Part of the time defending the pretend village or during our always useless raid on wagons was me choking an angry redneck child "on my side." I read about Quanah and found our purported genealogical link as a kid. Most paragraphs on his life described his blue eyes and dark skin and how he was "out for himself" as most half-breeds get accused of. I knew better. His blue eyes, in the black and white photograph made nearly white, told me they are out for you.

Even as the only kid the sun didn't turn red and burn in a single day, the North Texas or later the SoCal sun was too much after running around screaming bang bang! For guns and pffbt! For arrows. I'd say to a friend, let's go to your house and play GI Joe.

They'd tell me, as if it's a moral family choice to keep the house clean like taking off your shoes that, "My parents don't allow Mexicans inside." I tried to imagine how these conversations with their mom and dad might have happened. "Timmy no fighting or ruining your dinner when friends are over. And no wetback children, okay sweetie?" I mean, it's specific. When we lived in upper middle-class neighborhoods that were nearly all White, where my family was one of a handful of Brown families spread out, did they really expect there to be an epidemic of little cholos coming over their pristine white house no bigger than mine? No sugar plums in those parents' heads, but imaginary gangster kids with placa covered arms tagging Spanish cuss words all around and getting everyone pregnant.

For some friends there was no getting around it and the fathers and mothers were unapologetic about not letting me inside in the same manner they'd might tell you it's past your bedtime. Or they'd shout, "Out out out!" Like I was a possum or stray dog. In a reversal of the logic why I had to be the Indian, some friends would argue and say I was White, my last name was even Duncan...and sometimes it would work. "Okay don't let him wander. You guys only play in the living room." Other times, in between getting told to get outside and a friend whining no it's too hot, I myself with a burning face and skin would offer my last name was Duncan. I'd sell out to play GI Joe inside with my friends and to be treated as a person.

The No Mexicans Inside rule unsaid or to be determined in its application could be weird. Me and a friend already indoors moved on from GI Joe and would be quietly ramming Transformers together before their parents crept in. Fathers and mothers would see me and say, "…Oh," in a WASPy voice. They'd whisper and then come sit by us and ask me odd, serious questions. What does your momma look like? Where are your parents from? No, I mean before here. Well, where did your grandparents come from? I'd answer the odd questions not knowing they'd be the ones I'd hear every day of my life. The mother or father would either leave tired and confused or angrily blurt out, "When did you come from Mexico!!" More intent on Transformers I'd say, "Never, I think," because my grandparents insisted we were native to the Southwest, that we were hispanos—californios and nuevomexicanos—to me at a young age, but these parents didn't like the answer. I was supposed to be foreign and live on the other side of town or in a shelter. My father was supposed to work for them and be deferential and grateful. I was supposed to be the gateway for their offspring for drugs and violence. When my White father came to get me, there wasn't any confusion or problems. When my dark Brown mother came, the parents of friends were stiff and awkward. We weren't supposed to be there as equals.

My mother, child of the 60s and peripheral Chicano power slogans, would declare the thing, however true, her parents hated to hear, especially her mother with a Mission Indian father, that she—we—were Indians, though mom would say we were Spanish just as often. Then for the nice White family we were quaint. Tamed—house broken it seemed as we had already been killed outside by the hundreds in our game. In-between hearing, "Oh what tribe are you from?" and about the White parents' ubiquitous fake Cherokee princess grandmother, I wanted to shout. I wanted cowboys and frontier wives, my own people more than these wannabes, to squirm and die and lose. More than that, I wanted it to be okay for grandma and grandpa to speak Spanish better than English, that we ate cheese enchiladas instead of meatloaf, for us to be people and not entertainment. For us not to be a sideshow barometer for a fantasy connection to a land drenched in blood and death. Especially to those so vile to think a Mexican child could never be good enough to cross their threshold.

"Nu-uh!" Everyone stopped chatting and looked at the angry wild Brown kid.

"We're Mexican."

34.
True Son of Ramonaland: How to Spot a Real Californio

Much more worthy than the average Mexican, the noble *Californio* is nearly gone from their native land due to cross breeding and the inevitable, pre-ordained thrusting rise of the Anglo-Saxon. Weep not, pilgrims! It is but simple Darwinism, those bred in such an idyllic place cannot compete with those who arose in the icy forests of Europe.

As with Ramona, not all *Californios* are of the purest Spanish blood. Yet any perspicacious traveler can spot a true *Californio* by these signs gained from anthropology:

Two stomachs: as there was much grit in ranch life, one extra bovine stomach came in handy.

California shaped birthmark: Generations upon the land often produce an affinity or oneness with it that manifests in state outlines on backs or buttocks.

Tapping foot: as they are always ready to dance and make merry.

Resentment of the American: can you blame them? It is quite amusing to see their roosterish feathers rustled.

Fused teeth: an amazing adaptation to chewing on leather!

Bad eyesight: Does the noble Californio have any need to look beyond the fiesta of his own front porch?

Arm Flapping: The hardships of the people have led to many eccentricities.

Constellation of Beauty Marks: Oh, how many men wished to follow the line of marks that ran up and down Ramona's fair arms?

Affinity for animals: Californios adore animals much as Ramona did Baba the Horse or Capitán the Dog, also evidenced by her tender heartedness to her adopted Indian village.

35. Ramona Diary of SRD Entry: Beans Spotting

Riding the bus from the Estates outside town to school in town we saw the same guys our age everyone called illegals waiting for work every morning. The mist was heavy and it was hard to see them, jean-jacketed ghosts shuffling around. Soon the fog would burn off and they'd be jumping in a truck and going to work. Ray, the class clown, leaned out the bus window and shouted La migra! La migra! and the guys ran this way and that. The entire bus laughed, saying shit like he was scattering the beans. I told Ray that wasn't cool, we knew those guys and he said it was just a joke, he was down with the beaners. He said he was just Beans spotting.

In junior high Ray fought in one of the few race fights. Some White skaters and Mexican Americans were going to have a big brawl. Everyone called it, "The Bones Brigade versus the Beans Brigade." People were sweating me, "Are you going to the fight? Which side are you on?" Several of my friends were White skaters and punks. They were actually surprised I said I'd fight the asshole skaters, but that I wasn't going to because I wasn't going to get hit in the head with a skateboard. As they called me a scared queer, Ray proclaimed he was down with beaners, and he was fighting the Bones Brigade. They called me and him traitors, and he, according to what I heard, fought heroically, though I also heard he was the only one fighting, everyone else was just talking smack from far away. I thought both times, hearing about the fight and hearing him shout la migra on the bus, that "down with the gente" Whiteboys would be the death of me.

Every now and then from the bus we would see la migra actually putting everyone in a brown van. Big White guys in tight jeans and sunglasses speaking into walkie talkies. So many cops shove teenagers looking for work into vans. Another thing they did was buy kids booze, but that was good for me and my skate-punk friends. The first time I remember seeing the guys looking for work being shoved into the immigration van I didn't expect to see them again for a while. On the way back from school that afternoon, they were all back, waiting. I knew that getting back to where we lived had cost them, that they worked hard for what they had, and that running off to hide when kids yelled to make them look foolish could make them miss a job. Ray said he was down with beaners, but I swore that if he or anybody else on the bus tried shouting La Migra! La Migra! at them again, next time, I'd fight.

36.
Ramona Diary of SRD: Live Long and Pendejo

We—me and the Head Joaquin—finally got to Vasquez Rocks. Thanks to some helpful hippies in a creepy scarred vehicle that looked more like a kidnap van than free love-wagon, though it did reek of that greasy smell of mota. Three White guys with dreadlocks and tie-dyed shirts under saris or ponchos and one wore a dangly woven chullo. Walking patchworks dolls of cultural appropriations. One was named John, one called himself "Winter," and the last called himself, "Smiles," as in, "Nah man, not like Smiley. Just..." and he paused for a bit, "Smiles." They stunk of body odor and the aforementioned marijuana, but also of slumming middle-class runts rather than commune variety idealists. The stink I know so well being half White middle-class runt myself. Getting tattoos in unknown languages and ethnic beads, bangles, and other bullshit from far off lands and even those not so far off made by "native hands" ain't cheap, not to mention high quality tie-dyes and sarongs. Before I said anything about myself, they talked on and on about the moon and how like they really dig it and how they, "Just want to be free like you, bro, you know, and like, live off what this capitalistic society tosses away." They looked at me slyly for approval of their high-mindedness. They only saw my blank face as three thoughts came to me: One. How do they know I'm free? Two. I'm still way cleaner than they are, free or not. Three. Their granny didn't flee Europe to join in the exploitation of the people of Turtle Island so they would wind up becoming freegans.

The whole trip, I kept trying to calculate how much farther to Vasquez Rocks and then Joaquin would giggle out the word "pendejos" at them from my bag. The White hippies, thinking somehow that was my approval, would then all giggle in unison with approximate pronunciation of "pendejos." They must have thought it meant something approving or jolly rather than pubic hair, or a better translation, dumb asses. In my annoyance I recalled my knowledge of middle-class hippy clichés and asked, "What do your parents think about you guys, you know, being free?" It got real quiet then. The guy in the dangly yarn South American hat, wailed out, "My dad thinks I'm a loser." Soon they all were sobbing and trying to hug me, though this was all punctuated with Joaquin giggling out, "Pendejos," again, so the three hippies would cry snot bubbles and then laugh out the word, "¡Pendejos!" like it meant, "¡Viva!"

When we got to the trailhead of Vasquez Rocks, they said I was, "like connected, man" and they respected my wisdom. Smiles welcomed me to this country. I said, "Uh, okay, later, dudes," stepping down on sand and rocks. The driver, John or Winter, I don't know which, thumped his fist to his chest and mouthed the word, "Pendejos," to me, as if it meant, "Much love," before driving off.

Since it was already getting dark, we figured we wouldn't see these rocks until the morning…yet we headed up a bit and saw, with the splotches of stars already behind it, the crashed geologic rocket ship Vasquez Rocks.

"Big deal!" Joaquin said.

"Big deal? Tiburcio Vasquez hid out here. This is like the center of Chicanismo."

"Chickenismo? Sheesh, work on your pronunciation, vato, or I'll call you pendejo, too. You ain't here no for no chickenismo, anyway, you are just here for your TV shows. That Sun Walker, Moon Jumper, whatevers."

"*Star Trek.*"

"You've watched way too much TV, cabrón."

We sat on the trail and indeed stared at the rocks like they were television. Being a latch key kid raised by TV makes me need to decompress after dealing with people, even if it's socializing with pendejos.

These rocks were on all the old shows, so much I felt like we were on a production set. This wasn't only the place where Kirk fought the Gorn lizard on *Star Trek*. Vasquez Rocks show up on *Buck Rogers* and *Buffy*. That ex-Confederate, Indian robbing and killing John Carter in *John Carter* thought he was on Mars when he really was in California standing on these rocks. The rocks show up in Anglo Cowboy Jesus shows like *The High Chaparral* and even *Blazing Saddles*. Even Michael Jackson danced here. Zorro hid out here in that Disney show making everything weird, metafictional, commercial, which all sounds Californian as hell.

Joaquin asked me, "Why do you say this is the center? I don't see any gift shops."

"Vasquez hid out here so they got his name."

Joaquin then complained on and on about how no rocks were named for him.

"You got a book and a famous poem, man. Most people don't get that."

"He wasn't so cool! I'm the cool one."

"Vasquez was a Californio well known by other Californios. You were a bandido from Sonora who wasn't here too long. Makes sense he got some rocks."

"You don't know! I'm the center of chickenismo! Carajo, you got me saying it now."

"Tiburcio also said for fifty thousand dollars, he could have got arms and a force to revolutionize California. What did you say, Joaquin?"

"Madre de Dios. You know a lot for a coconut. I knew all these guys! Vasquez! That one other guy. And what's his name too! I was like their padre. What did Captain Vader say, I am your father? That."

"If you are Joaquin Murrieta. You might be some guy that got caught."

Joaquin then went on and on about how he was indeed the real Joaquin, the only one, and how he was the middle chicken, as he forgot what we were speaking about Chicanismo rather than poultry.

Not for the first time I felt like kicking his glass jar off a cliff and watching his head smash in a puff of glass and whisky. Instead, I said, "Why are we fighting?"

"I'm sorry pocho. For real, cabròn. I am demoting you though. A squabble between bandits in arms is nothing, but you have yet to prove yourself."

I didn't want to remind Joaquin I had proven myself in his eyes and he told me now that I would be labeled something like a getaway horse, as I was his primary means of locomotion.

We stared at the blackening rocks and the sparkling spaceship in the warp night sky.

"If all those TVs shows were here, how come they never filmed Tiburcio?"

"No TV back then and this was just a hiding spot."

I stopped myself.

Maybe Tiburcio was still here. Still hiding, fighting, resisting. On TV.

He was a part of a TV ritual narrative and these rocks are the stage.

He was necessary to make the viewers know who and what they are—American. Those who have vanquished, tamed, "civilized" a continent. Those who destroyed us. They put Joaquin's head on display. Likewise, the defeat of Tiburcio is on display every Friday night or down streaming 24/7.

We are the Gorn lizards to be overcome, the braves to be killed, the zombies to be shot. Tiburcio underneath all the CGI costumes.

The White heroes fight him, the monstrous other, laying horrors of their innards upon his character, not letting him rest in peace, resurrecting him again and again to kill him on TV. Now I'm glad that it was Winter, John, and Smiles rather than *Star Trek* nerds that we got a ride from. Pendejos are preferable to phasers set to kill at high noon.

I had been talking aloud or Joaquin can hear everything I think now.

"He is the monster in the rubber suit! We are mutantes!"

"The monster experiment they can't handle!" I laughed.

"Hey, take it easy, carnal, we weren't invented by no English lady."

"What, do you mean, *Frankenstein*?"

I forgot he was the Night of the Living Head in a whisky jar that I trot around California.

Joaquin's trout pseudoscience eyes on fire. "¡Yo no soy pinche Frakenstein!"

Our discussion was like a commercial. We were back at Vasquez Rocks TV.

Joaquin sighed loudly. He tilted up in his container, angling to see past the crest of the whiskey that filled two thirds of the jar. "These rocks ain't too bad, Sr. Horse." He gazed at the *Star Trek*-like backdrop and the space rock fingers pointing forward, adelante. "We mutantes are still here. Maybe we can get this rocket ship going."

37.
Ramona Diary of SRD: None of My Friends Drive a Low-rider

My first car when I was eighteen was a 1963 Cadillac Fleetwood. My White father bought it from an old lady who had kept it in her garage. Everything was great—power windows, power steering, power fins—except for the paintjob. I never had enough money or interest in cars to paint it right. I could barely afford gas in the monster, which kept me close to home, which is what my dad wanted.

Owning and driving this car, my White boy disguise of White name and not speaking Spanish blew off in the wind. I was Brown, the car was old, so the car had to be a low-rider. Little Anglo-Saxon children asked me to pump the hydraulics as I waited at red lights. They also asked me if I had any weed. White friends told me I should put the Virgin Mary on the hood. I asked them don't you put the Virgin Mary on your crappy car? They wouldn't answer. The police pulled me over at least once a week yelling, "WHAT ARE YOU DOING IN THIS NEIGHBORHOOD, SPIC!" Living here was never good enough, I had to be some "vato" dealing to little White kids or getting White girls hooked so I could be their pimp. I'd get pulled out of the car like it was on fire, get tossed against the back door and then the cop would press up against me like a dirty pedo mall Santa and smash my genitals in their pat down. "Fuck tha Police" by N.W.A. echoed in my mind along with the thought "Damn, it's real."

When they took a look at my license my White name superpower kicked in. The cop's voice changed, and they thanked Mr. Duncan for his time. I got to know every gringo cop in town by name and we'd still go through the same line of questions till they got to my magic card. I could see the moment inside their head when wetback gangbanger turned to, Oh, Mr. Duncan. Thank you for your time. They had approached me with guns drawn, called me spic, demanded to know where I hid the drugs and the guns, then ask if I spoke English after ten minutes of speaking English, but my card worked every time because of the gift of a northern European name from my father and not Juan Bautista after my grandfather.

The magic failed around the same time my power steering went out. Luckily, the roads in Dallas are uniform and straight as it took all my strength to turn the tank I was driving. When a friend of mine named David from Belize (not the only other Mexican in school from my childhood David) and I watched movies until four a.m., he got tired and complained about wanting to go home, so I decided to take him back. Around five a.m., the streets were empty, and we were still technically in my suburb, and not yet to Dallas. A cop followed us for a while and then turned on his lights. I kept wondering if you can get a ticket for no power steering and saw that I didn't know this cop, he was young.

"What are y'all doing in this neighborhood?"

"Taking this guy home."

"So y'all been up all night doing drugs."

"What? We don't do drugs, we were watching movies."

"What movies?"

"*Phantom of the Opera* with Freddy Krueger, and *Graffiti Bridge* with Prince."

"Let me see your identification."

Normally they asked later, after the car slam, a few more spics out their mouths, and a harsh genital smash, so I looked at him a moment before I reached down for my wallet in my chinos and the cop had his gun half way out and said, "If you pull out anything but a wallet, you and me are gonna tango." My friend snickered at "tango."

"It's just a wallet." I saw his gringo King Arthur facing the wetback dragon eyes and moved slow. He wanted an excuse to end his fear. That could have been me, dead at eighteen, and I wondered something I always wonder when the police point guns at me that I told my dad later.

I gave him the magic card, but the magic fizzled and he told me to get out of the car slowly and stand by the trunk.

"So you were doing drugs."

"No."

"Then why are your eyes red?"

"I'm tired. I've been up watching movies."

David bolts out of the car, arms raised, saying what the hell, both me and the cop yell at him to get back in, and he's like what the hell I can do what I want. I tell the cop he's a foreigner and doesn't know any better and David says fuck you man and finally gets back in. The cop asked me questions trying to trip me up and asked if I'm a citizen, like they always do.

"Well, I got a license and a social security card in my wallet."

He was way shorter than me, like most of them were, but he tried to buck up and stare me down. He asked like Dirty Harry what they all asked, what was he going to find in the trunk. I said what I always say: get a warrant, I'll wait. I didn't have a Brown father for the talk, but I learned quickly that cops don't like following the law, so I always ask for a warrant.

"What would the dogs find when I do?"

"I don't know, get your dogs. I got time."

This cop scared the shit out of me because he was scared and on his own and didn't see us, only saw Scarface and Danny Trejo as Gangbanger #1. We were freshman college kids who didn't even smoke mota. I wanted a warrant. I wanted him to call for other cops that might manhandle us, but maybe would hold him back or witness our murder. We were near the huge cemetery my White grandmother was buried in and it was still late or early and no one was around. King Arthur Cop could shoot us both and plant whatever he wanted in our dead hands.

When he lets me go he tells me he pulled me over for swerving in the lane, which was impossible with power steering out. As we drove off, David said he wanted to ice that rookie and that I should get him fired, that this shit wouldn't happen in Belize. I wanted to do something, but I knew better than to try. Like my Belizean friend didn't know the police here only saw us as monsters, my White friends and family don't believe someone can be pulled over, hassled, dirty Santa felt up, or shot for just being Brown, or even kinda Brown like me.

Later that day when I told my father and his brother, they only said, "The officer was doing his job," and, "I might have done the same."

"What if he killed me?" I kept asking my uncle, he never answered or swerved from the righteousness of cops. I knew from his many pontifications that he thought police were meant to keep Blacks and Mexicans in the hood and the barrio. It hurt when he, the only one who took me in when my parents neglected me, said me and my friend David whom he hugged all the time deserved it because we don't fit the demographics for this neighborhood.

Dad paused his "police, right or wrong" speech when I asked what if I died. I told him whenever the cops drew guns I wondered what the papers would say if they killed me. Would I be a good White boy going to college or just a criminal beaner who had it coming? And would it take me having a White father to have justice? Would the tears of my Brown family mean so little?

We never talked about it, how people who love me disbelieve my experience or love the system that benefited them their entire lives too much to doubt it, again and again.

The next weekend I asked my White friends if we could ride in their car and leave mine at home and told them what always happens when they asked why. They said I have to expect it in that car.

"What car?"

"A low-rider."

38.
Ramona Diary of SRD: The Blinking Giant of Shanghai

The hotel room was like all the cookie-cutter American ones I had stayed in, except the giant city of Shanghai blinked in the night outside its window. When I arrived, my lack of a sense of direction allowed me to dare only a block in each direction from the hotel's main doors before running back to my room. I didn't want to get lost in the ancient alley mazes or endless modern facades and miss my flight to the interior of the country the next day, after all. This was the first truly foreign country I had been to since Mexico and England share plenty with the Southwest. That said, Shanghai seemed rather normal yet ultra-modern despite the anachronisms in the cracks and corners. No one had three arms and two heads, of course, and I was quite used to hearing half-understood languages around me.

Laying there in a very new place I had come to live, to teach, I thought of my first night living in Texas at my Uncle Billy Bob's (yes, his real name) house, missing the cold coyote-filled California night. But now I also missed the howl of trains as well as those of the wild dogs. I would find in China that the Chinese would insist I wasn't American and the Europeans I worked with would tell me I seemed American, why did I want to be Mexican, of all things? Neither knew history or the existence of Chicanos or the assimilation we are subjected to if we want to do more than just get by. They expected the Frito Bandito.

For expediency, I would tell the Chinese my father was American and my mother Mexican. They then would sneer and tell me Mexicans are lazy. It would take me aback, and I'd say well I am, but how'd you know? And had they ever met a Mexican? I knew most of the people who said that had only seen one half a Mexican, and a pocho coconut one too at that, namely me. I didn't hold it against my Chinese friends who said this, who also tended to say you are handsome or fat in the same friendly, yet brusque manner. I figured out why they had this attitude towards a people they had never seen—Anglos export their racism. The lazy Mexican stereotype comes from American writings and representations of Mexican California and the Californios, my own ancestors. They described a rich land governed and misused by a lazy, indolent, and mongrel people who let the Indians do all the work (something the Americans took over and added in their institutions of native slavery and genocide). A land ripe for plundering. And all the racist justifications for the invasion like "Lazy Mexicans" still exist as they lend a sense of superiority to the Anglo imagination and justify their having while others have not. Those from overseas who come to the states or get Anglo-centric information disseminated in English don't want to ally their mental space with the losers, those subject to racism and portrayed so poorly, but with those who benefit from the system the most, whether the paternalistic love the dark children liberal or kill 'em all redneck.

Not to say other cultures don't come with their own bag about light and dark and who should do all the shit work. I was just surprised that even in the absence of any Mexicans the Chinese would agree that shit work should be done by Mexicans.

While I was privileged in China and loved the Chinese savoir faire, I didn't know laying there in the hotel room in the sight of the blinking giant of Shanghai, missing cold nights and coyotes while intrigued by mega cities and rickshaws, that there, of all places at the other end of the Pacific, a place I had dreamed of since standing on the beach in LA as a kid, that my Native American blood would mark me again in the eyes of others as a lesser being.

39.

True Son of Ramonaland: Ramona's Kissing Tree

Background

While there are many places that purport to possess the tree under which Allesandro and Ramona first kissed, this kissing tree, though nowhere near a ranch and not in a garden as described in the book, is the most famous and hence the most authentic. All the great Californians were conceived here since the air of romance that pervades this area became known and described through Helen Hunt Jackson's fabulous book. Patton's parents consummated their marriage right here. On the way to the valley, Caesar Chavez's parents had a romantic picnic.

The famous Kissing Tree, however, has long since been felled, but the view and romantic stump remain. As with many famous places in California, the area has its origins as an ancient native refuse heap. Don't be surprised once you are taken over by the romance of the stump when, as you lay your loved one down for a cuddle, he or she yelps in pain and finds a jagged pot shard embedded in the back.

Many movies, though not connected with Ramona, have used this area as a site for a teenage make out session followed by a traditional Californian thrill kill. The stump is also famed as the "drop site" in the cult film *Big Hook*. Do not be alarmed by a spattering of counterculture types lingering at the altar of their masterpiece, as the stump has become a popular hangout spot for movie aficionados and has become as recognizable as Vasquez Rock on TV. In consideration for this movie and the social ills it describes and the likelihood for a pure Ramonan pilgrim to rub shoulders with the vagabonds who have overtaken our sacred spot for their own devices, we include this special note.

Zorro's Note—Not My Little Girl:

Fathers—Your little girl, whatever her age, may well fall under the spell of the Latin Guapo, some slick black-haired wolf who would take advantage of her. Whether it is on her own accord to rebel against your dominion, or the Latinate glamor takes her, the coupling of your daughter with a Latino man is nothing a parent should live through. An inexperienced girl needs to be told that the stain of the Brown wolf might indeed rub off and she'll find herself the mother of a litter of Spanish eyed cubs, her "Guapo" nowhere to be seen. Or she could be found walking the streets just to get another hit of Mary Jane or worse from a swarthy pimp.

Behavior to watch out for:

*Majoring in Spanish

*Posters of movies stars with suspicious names

*Spanish Language Music or so-called Musica

*Latina Friends, who will definitely be in a gang and into drugs

*Being on the soccer team, which combines all the warning signs into one

Hints and Tips

Due to increasing government costs and to prevent overtime pay, no law enforcement officers will perform the traditional knock on the window and issuing of indecency citations. However a statue of a blushing officer wagging his finger located in the center of the outlook may suffice for your needs.

Additionally, Zorro implores you to watch out for serial killers. This is California, famed home of murderers and the deranged.

40.

The Ramona Diary of SRD: I Blame Olivia Newton John

I kinda hooked up. Also, everyone thinks I'm a serial killer now. It all started with Head Joaquin demanding that I find him a place to sleep that, "befit his station." He said he had enough of camping, which is what he called our destitute rambles through the dry hills of Southern California. I kept him, which means the jar that holds his head, in the dark of my backpack. So, as I came upon a parking lot, I said aloud, "Hello Mr. Hotel Attendant, I'm traveling with the renowned head of Joaquin Murrieta, so I will require your best room." I then mimicked a hotel clerk and said, "Yes, sir, what an honor! May we speak with the famous Chicano folk hero?" I said, "No, he does not wish to be disturbed by plebeians such as yourself." I then messed up and said in my own voice, "Well, maybe next time. The luxury suite is right through here, sir." I lay down between two cars and used my diary as a pillow. I heard Joaquin say, "Finally I'm getting treated like I deserve." And I thought, money saved, you jerk.

The two cars we were between rocked heavily and I instinctively jumped up and looked for the doorway that wasn't there. My foot then kicked Joaquin's jar, which spun and crashed against the curb. His head rolled in a puddle of whiskey and broken glass. I bravely ran through the earthquake and scooped him up into a plastic shopping sack from my pocket. I then braced for ground fissures, falling buildings, anything, but the ground was still and even, and only the cars rocked and I saw their windows were steamy. Just another sexually generated earthquake. I worried about Joaquin and his lack of whiskey, which has preserved him for a century and a half and of course mollifies him. Joaquin screamed, "Ugh, what's up with this crap hotel?!" and then said, like he always says, that he needed a better sidekick.

I hoped the people having public sex had alcohol for Joaquin. Maybe I was wrong for bothering them. The correct form of address in certain social situations confuses me and asking something from someone engaged in public sex is one of them. I stood a bit too embarrassed to knock on the steamy window for a moment too long. A dark-haired woman wiped a circle. She was nude and I couldn't help looking which made me pause another moment in which she saw Joaquin's face pressed against the plastic of the bag. She screamed really loud.

Behind me, which must have been the people in the other car, I heard, "Shit shit shit, oh my God start the car Brock!" I gave up on asking for booze and ran. Then engines and headlights. I saw I had chosen to sleep in a make-out spot, not just a parking lot, and now I was in a stage light with my human head in a bag. Most of the cars squealed to get out of there, but one bastard rammed me at low speed. Head Joaquin and I rode the hood TJ Hooker style which isn't as fun as you think. I saw the driver's window open and swung the plastic bag with Joaquin's head against his. The bash did the trick to make him stop, but when I landed on the hard parking lot gravel, it felt like I was the one who head butted the yuppie driving with no shirt and no pants.

I lay achy on the ground, hoping if I stayed still life would get better. Joaquin started his moaning again, how he needed to stop hanging out with half-breeds like me. At least the public sex people were all gone.

Then this White girl. She came from the bushes behind me and had her pretty face in mine. She said stuff like, "You okay? What was all that about? Where did my ride go?"

I told her I recently acquired a historic artifact and people are scared of it sometimes.

She sat down. She told me she was out "with some guy" and he was gone after she came back from the bathroom. Her name was Brenda, Linda, something and I told her everything. About Ramona—No, the book, not the play! About getting Joaquin Murrieta's head and how I'm reclaiming my Californio inheritance. I might have sounded a little militant which is embarrassing around White people, but they are the ones always around, though they never seem to notice the militant stuff anyway.

We gathered the dribbles inside liquor bottles to put inside the plastic sack that now held Joaquin. She told me wished she was mixed-race because she was just normal. I wondered if she had listened to what I said, but then she said Latin guys are hot, which took things an entirely different route.

Maybe she was impressed by my knowledge of local history, which seems unlikely, but I intend to try it out on more women to see. Just then though, I wasn't really in the mood, but I couldn't say no to her: I blame Olivia Newton John for imprinting on me at an early age. *Grease* had just come out and our TV filled up with her pale sculptured face in disco sparkles and stiff hair sprayed blond hair. She went from a tight leather suit that held the mysteries of adulthood to impossible tighter yoga pants and promises in heavy black lined blue-eyed looks and hot pink lips. Now I can't say no to blond women who look like they are about to do Jazzercise, no matter how they get on my nerves, which Brenda Linda Something did by asking me again and again what my real name was even though I kept saying, "Scott Duncan! It's Scott Duncan!" And then she said:

"You're like the best of both worlds, I can tell my father you're White and tell my mother you're Mexican. Mexican guys are so hot."

After that I was just quiet. I don't know what to say to things like that. Oh, your parents are racists, how nice. You like sex with Mexican men. How egalitarian.

Brenda, Linda's pink and blue Memphis Group patterned jogging tights almost hidden by her oversized hoody weren't the haloed disco gown of Xanadu, but were on theme for ONJ's later workout songs. Fast forward to her calling a cab and between that and the motel went my money, till later when I rifled her wallet at the urging of Joaquin who insisted esta loca should be paying us.

In the motel room, we got to kissing, my skin jumping and eager, but then she held me back.

"Call me a whore in Spanish."

"What? Why?"

"It's what I like. I want him to watch too." Him being Head Joaquin.

I thought I'd throw her a bone and combed my brain for hija de puta's and perra's and hoped she'd forget about Head Joaquin. I wondered if I could perform sexually with an audience since I can't even pee with one. In the end, she made me set him on the nightstand, Head Joaquin's eyes already bugged out at her lithe but shapely form.

"Chingame," she said, "Is that right?" Then she said it again. Joaquin neck-snailed along the table towards her. "¡Yo soy el primero Joaquín! El actual. Este puto es Medio Güero Joaquín solamente."

"That's hot, so fucking hot." She smooched Joaquin's zombie lips. A deflating event and so I figured I'd just leave, but then her pretty blue eyes looked at me through the mud mask of dead Joaquin's smear. I don't know what she said next for sure. It might have been, "Let's do it, beautiful," or "That tastes miserable," or "Let's see that tentacle," but what I heard was, "Let's get physical."

And with that one perhaps imagined Olivia reference, my body was not my own, but some bucking mule's back my brain was riding. A horrible night followed with me striving to put Joaquin back on the nightstand, or at least out of sight as Brenda, Linda, Something and I fornicated. And she instead would get on all fours and demand I debase her further en español while she clutched Head Joaquin, performing what I'll call necklingus. She'd say, "Call me a pretty bitch" I'd say, "Linda perra." "Tell me to mow my own damn yard." I would shout limpiar and mumble a bit. I really reached the limits of my disgust tolerance and Spanish ability.

I would also throw in Qué tetonas! Qué culo! at random, hoping it would keep her from asking me to say anything too difficult, but towards the end she asked me to call her something so vile, long, and complicated that I won't write it down. I had no idea how to translate it, so I linked up random Spanish words. Nota especial frijoles lado santos chinos cuminos verdes playas patas. It thrilled her.

When it was all said and done, we both were covered in bits of Joaquin's ancient, pickled flesh and our own love juices. She kissed me deep with tongue and I remembered too late her necklingus with Joaquin. I cleaned my tongue with a pillow when she said I was so macho, taking what I wanted, though she was the one yelling stick this, spank that, and roll your r's. I curled up with the sheets, cringing at her appetite for debasement as well as my own willingness to go along, though this was not the first time I've experienced such things from a White girl, just the first time with a decapitated head in the mix.

As I lay in the sex crater next to her, I thought grandma wasn't right. I don't need to stay away from all White girls, just the crazy ones, though most seem into weird gangsta or boss's daughter fantasies. Or is it me? How can a gringa be exotic to me, though, as someone who mostly grew up in White neighborhoods. Also, I didn't just like Oliva as a kid, I liked Linda Carter, Donna Summer, and plenty of other beautiful Brown stars on TV and posters. Maybe I've just been the contact point for a fantasy.

Meanwhile, Head Joaquin, Chicano hero, California rebel, teetered on the edge, completely forgotten by Brenda, Linda, Something and was about to fall over. I picked him up, saving him from yet another head bash.

He said, "About time you got me laid, güero." I put him in a boozy mix and tied the plastic shopping bag real tight, though I knew it wouldn't shut him up. "Glad you're finally acting like a man."

I don't know if I got him laid, or he got me laid, but I felt like I needed to leave. But, because I was tired and enjoyed having a mattress over a parking lot, I watched TV from the bed. On the news, as the reporter yakked, came up a blurry cell phone picture of my grimy face grimacing and holding Head Joaquin above the words KILLER "TWO-HEADS" ON THE LOOSE. That's when I left. Because if that's how freaky Brenda, Linda, Something got when she was having sex with a Mexican, Lord knows what she'd do with a serial killer.

41.
Ramona Diary of SRD: How I Learned I'm a Wetback

The Duncan side of the family owned a store in Dallas by White Rock Lake: a convenience store that they call the "Bait Shop," referencing its original merchandise, despite its giant sign that says DUNCAN'S. And the area around the store my family calls "The Hill," though I as a Californian could never find any hills there. My Dad and Uncle Billy Bob (yes his real name as I always have to say) often described "The Hill" as a den of iniquity and how once before it might have made for a good novel, but by the time I was a kid, that time had passed. Yet, Dad still took me there. So, when I was three, it was at "The Hill" that I learned the word wetback from my family and, moreover, that wetback meant me.

I liked the Bait Shop as a kid, though. They had candy and comics and I got a discount. I also liked the freezer and the smell of refrigeration, though I disliked the stink of puddled beer that came from the back of the store. Dad's cousin ran the bait shop, and though he lacked the Duncan ruddiness that either comes from a gallon of Scottish Picts or pint of Comanche, he shared Dad's eyes and eyebrows, the same eyebrows as mine. He was also rude as hell to Blacks and Mexicans, though he always had a Mexican slave to run to and fro carrying boxes. I recall him telling Black people to get out many times or him talking about "fucking wetbacks" as groups of Mexicans approached the shop, during their purchase, and as they left.

At three, I had already forgotten and been reintroduced to my Mexican side of the family, though it could have only been a month or two since I left LA. My Aunt Linda told me who everyone was as they burst into our house in Texas for a visit, including who she was, but she looked like a slightly fairer, curlier version of mom, so I took her word that she was my mother's sister. I asked her why everyone sounded funny, which meant the Spanglish and the Chicano English. She told me because they were Mexican.

"Am I one too?"

"Yes, m'ijo yes!"

Then I became reacquainted with grandma, who had a plate of cheese enchiladas out of nowhere. With everyone hugging and being loud and joking and with my doting grandmother and a plate of enchiladas, being Mexican wasn't half bad. I was only three and I already liked it.

When the people left the bait shop and my Dad's cousin said, "Those fucking wetbacks," to one of my White uncles, I knew they were talking about them and it wasn't something good, but I didn't know what it meant. By the other side of the cash machine, I looked up at them. "What does wetback mean?" I said it several times. Dad's cousin kind of looked away and got a little red. My uncle looked down at me and drawled, "It's someone who crossed a border." I repeated his definition to him. "That's it," he told me.

They talked on about wetbacks and I looked through the window of the freezer door at the Mexican worker stacking boxes who looked like the guys they called wetback, who looked like my mom's side, who looked like me. I knew that wetback was supposed to be a detestable thing and that it meant them and that it meant me.

42.
Ramona Diary of SRD: L.A. Migra

Just passing through, heading towards L.A. Unfortunately, in the Southwest, that means moving through border patrol stops miles from any border. I worried about the contraband I had: an old flintlock, a few oranges, and a human head.

As a teenager I used to travel from Texas to California often. La Migra always stops me, always tells me that my ID is probably stolen and waits there. They are always "just doing their job," and after the first few times, I realized that their job was to hassle Brown people, no matter which side of the border they lived on. It made me wonder where the border is when they check this far north of Mexico.

Old hippies in front of me were whining down by the curb from where they were made to sit.

"Come on man, we didn't do nothing. We're just, you know, living, man."

I was walking by the agent pulling Mexicans out of the hippies' trunk when he yelled, "Hey where'd you come from?" I kept walking but he yelled stop. "You didn't get out of this car did you?" I just said it wasn't illegal to walk. I also realized I had no ID—Head Joaquin's cretin gang of Joaquins took my wallet from me when they took me to see him.

"Hey, where you from?"

"Walking through."

"I can see that smart ass."

"Where you from?"

I glared at him. Texas winter White had turned to California redwood brown. Hanging out with 19th century undead and scratching the land for same century artifacts had made me look like a cross between an old frontiersman and a 21st century bum. I now had a floppy hat, and an empty bandolier. My sneakers and broken specs, the only thing modern that I retained.

"Speak English?"

"Yeah, and I'm from here." And speaking English as always with authorities.

"Where's here?"

"You should know where you are standing."

"You American or Mexican?"

I reached deep in my bag. I felt Ramona coins and some dirt. Then a card, which must have fallen out of my wallet. "Here you go."

"This is fake. It's a crime to misrepresent your citizenship."

"No, it's a real go-cart license. I'm a citizen of Race Town Speedtrack."

He grunted. "What's in that bag comedian? Open it up."

I held the flap of the bag open, showing the top of Joaquin's jar.

He tapped the jar.

"What's this, pickles?"

"No."

"Hogshead?"

"Nah."

"What you got in there? Better not be out of state produce or it'll be your ass."

I pulled down the bag a little farther down the face of the jar. Joaquin blinked at him through the boggy booze.

"It's Two-Heads! The killer! It's Two-Heads!"

L.A. Migra went for irons, pulled up too quickly, and shot his knee.

A couple other interior border agents started firing, not at me, but at the desert, the highway, the sky. The buzz of gunshots didn't bother me so much as this is America and concerts, high school, hunting trips to West Texas, and the police had prepared me well to react to gun play. The two hippies got up and jumped back in their car. Their trunk was wide open and I hopped in.

I closed the top just enough to see, indeed we were not followed and yes, L.A. Migra were shooting at each other, proving themselves to be the elite guardians of American borders. As the car sped off, in the dark of the trunk, after I felt myself for holes and had a small argument with Joaquin after he asked why I was always running like a chicken-shit, I realized I was being smuggled into the city my ancestors created before there was a city or the ideas of the nations of Mexico or the USA, on a coast some of them lived for thousands of years before that. Where I was born. Los Angeles.

43.
Ramona Diary of SRD: Fall of Some Californios

The floor drooped like a cereal bowl. So much so that crashing below and dying in the debris always came to mind while on the couch watching *ThunderCats* at 5 pm before anyone else got home.

We were the only Chicano family living in the Estates and now we were the only White family living in our run-down apartment complex in Ramona the town, though we were as dark as everyone else, and mom was usually darker.

In Texas, re-experiencing winter, my face and arms faded to what I call almond meat White. It was a shock because until then I thought of myself as redwood brown. People stay outdoors more in Southern California, especially me as my outdoor haunts; the dam, the rock, the hole, were my places of safety. In Texas it was my room in my uncle's house: dark and barricaded against the sun.

Why our ethnicity changed in town, of course, was because of the neighbors. When they're White we're Mexicans, when they're Brown we are in the door. I imagine, however, living in the complex where all the broke-ass Mexicans lived permanently settled most people's idea of what we were. Dad wasn't around, but we still had his last name to confuse people a bit.

Our nice furniture crowded together in the shitty apartment. It looked like an antique shop or a nutty old lady's apartment. And in ways it was both. The furniture was a remnant of a more economic and familial stable age. Mom was just as controlling as Señora Moreno from *Ramona,* the novel, and likewise it was as easy to escape from our apartment in Ramona the town as Ramona herself escaped the ranch.

I came home drunk a few times. My mother, too indifferent to notice, but my sister's friend Candy that I and my friends would spy upon in better days when we had the pool caught us smoking and saw our meager petty stash. (More accurately I spied on her, my friends would spy on both and I would hit them when I saw their eyes go to my sister.) She said, "Finally me and your sister can stop hiding what we do." I wondered what the hell that was, but I was gone to Texas before anything else I did or she did came to light.

It was strange that the loss of affluence gave us greater access to amenities. A grocery store, a radio shack, and a pizza place we had no money for were at the corner. Vandalism and thievery weren't as cool as it was in junior high or I would have gone wild. The loss of wildlife pushed me to change my ways—I learned to watch people going about their business instead of hawks, rattlesnakes, and gophers.

Despite being broke, despite hating my mother, I was doing well. By the time we lived in town, I was used to no money, little food, and crazy outbursts. Living in Ramona, the town was okay. It might have from been living near other Brown folk, but the fall of some Californios, for once, wasn't as bad as it could have been.

44.

The Ramona Diary of SRD: My Heart is Bathed in Chilis

The first time I had real hot peppers, a part of me died. Home was virtually a pepper-free zone as my Chicano mother only ate pickled jalapeños whose vinegar I found unappealing and my White father made a pico de gallo he called hot sauce, which I would later call Anglo-sauce. Yet I saw hot pepper consumption often since I stayed every summer with my grandparents in LA. We'd eat over at my Aunt Linda's and everyone would dump hot sauce over everything at breakfast and every time I would ask, "Is there any ketchup?" for me and my sister, Aunt Linda would look at me. "I don't know," eyes wide, "Hey Rebecca! is there any ketchup left over from when you dated that guy? The gringo?"

"You mean Steve?"

"Yeah." My cousin Rebecca would then bring the year-old ketchup bought for some polite and terrified White boyfriend for our eggs or potatoes. All eyes would be on me and my sister in our ketchup shame. Grandma would stare at the globs on our plate and say, "You going to eat that?" My uncle would say, "I think they are." My sister, Clara, the tougher one, would glare back at our family saying, "We like ketchup!"

And everyone would purse their lips and say, "We gotta do something about how White you kids are."

I met my chili pepper death after one of those ketchup shame breakfasts. I walked into the kitchen and saw my Uncle Joe sweating and holding on to the counter. He was eating chips and heaps of salsa. "Is it good?" I asked him. He wiped the side of his face. "Oh, it's good," he sputtered. "Your grandma made it."

There was no place safer than a kitchen with my grandmother and nothing more inert than the only homemade salsa I knew, dad's Anglo-sauce. I ate some of grandma's salsa, a big some.

And then I thought I had slurped nail polish remover. It was like drinking the whiskey from the jar that holds Joaquin Murrieta's head. And years later when I saw the crapola movie *Interview With a Vampire* and Brad Pit gets bitten in the graveyard and yelps and the world goes gray before it becomes hyper-rainbow real...I thought, hey that was how eating my first hot peppers was. Vampirism must be easy.

But then at my first real hot pepper hit, the chilis took the slow bus down my throat and got off in my chest. I looked at my grandmother, whose name Mercy seemed ironic, and asked, "Why? Why grandma why?"

Grandma Mercy, washing a pot, called over, "Don't blame me, 'Cotty, your uncle likes it."

I, too, held the edges of the counter, dreading the mass of chilis ever hitting my stomach. Yet the chilis never made it there and instead settled on my heart. The chilis consumed the slow vivid world, and then, consumed my heart itself. And I loved them.

My uncle patted my back, now as sweaty as his face. "We are burning the White boy out of you, m'ijo."

And ever since then, chili peppers have been my vampire blood and air. And often my heart burned because of disappointments and indignations, but all the fires felt like chili pepper fire. Books I read seemed to describe this burning. Seguin, the Tejano hero of the Revolution who was later robbed of everything by the very Texans he fought for, warned Chicanos that we would be treated as foreigners in our own land. Montezuma, writhing in his palace in Tenochtitlan, said it better as an Aztec city fell under Cortez—"My heart is bathed in chilis." Dissatisfied and disenfranchised hearts burn. My heart burns because 1846 has never ended. My heart burns because I'm still seen as a descendant of Cain, who we know from trash romance novels is our vampire father, but really means I am a native of Turtle Island. My heart burns because I have survived here, in the place of many fires, the dry kindling of my homeland of the Southwest.

I have changed many to my side, to chili vampirism. They sweated and burned as I had, till they saw the world anew with chili pepper eyes. If you love me, you love chili peppers. Montezuma's chili swishing heart. My own spicy heart.

45.

Ramona Diary of SRD: A Portrait of The Battle of San Pasqual with My Cat Pickles

Center: The Hero:

Modeled after me of course (who is writing this?). I am the focus, less tan than normal, it is winter, December 6th, after all. My brown hair flows behind, I have a little goatee that was popular at the time of the battle and when I was in high school, when I was unable or unwilling to grow one and look like a pirate. I have a straight brimmed sombrero cordobés much like the one Zorro sports but decorated with silver and turquoise. My mouth is set in grim determination. Eyes are big and wild, yet the artist (I'm thinking Titian) took care to paint White spots to connote plastic highlights of my contacts, which, despite flying dirt and blood splatter, would be better for such a close quarters horsey combat of San Pasqual than my oft repaired spectacles.

Center top: They called themselves los galgos, the Greyhounds:

Along the center, to the top and fading are a small group of Californio riders in their button up pants and flat-topped hats. There were only eighty of them versus several hundred Bear Flaggers and soldiers.

A great great, perhaps great or another great uncle was there at San Pasqual. At the battle site museum, there was a kindly docent dressed in vaquero regalia who pointed to me the handwritten list by Pico. How much I liked him though he was cast as the villain and not the center of the story in the park skit and moreover as a "Mexican soldier" rather than local Californio rancher who may have just been involved in a rebellion against Mexico proper. Almost all of the small number of soldiers had been recalled and only a few who might have technically deserted Mexico but not the defense of California stayed. One such boy, a corporal in the army, organized and retook Los Angeles before the battle of San Pasqual and, like Luke and Han after blowing up the Death Star, became a general. The men listed at San Pasqual were more akin to the legendary portrayal of Minute Men rather than soldiers. On the list with fancy curved handwriting is a Verdugo. I'm not sure how the breakdown of relation to him is or if the Estradas listed might be related to my Soboba side as that is a common name. The Verdugos are a big family and were even then in the 1840s. Yet, who knows, the certain flash of eyes or curl of lip like mine might have actually been there at the battle.

I don't know how my more immediate family viewed the US invasion or if they took up arms against the more powerful foe of US professional soldiers with modern arms. I don't blame those on the fence or those drinking the Kool-Aid that the US might be better, especially as their Federalist rebellion was fueled by what the US revolutionaries wrote (not what they practiced). A Verdugo there at San Pasqual lets me say we didn't give in. Overwhelmed and divided amongst ourselves, we resisted.

Center below: The Mount:

Pickles' fluffy tabby fur is regal and her forepaws are drenched in blood and half a bear flagger dangles from her fanged mouth and the other half is stepped upon her right paw. Her eyes are wild in blood lust. Her hair is more on end and it seems as if she has many tails as the artist has decided to use license to convey her angry tail flicking (here at the mount we switch up artists to Frank Frazetta to convey Conan the Barbarian musculature and Heavy Metal darkness). The saddle is ornate, the horn is the carved head of an eagle, the wings spread backwards to form the seat. The bridle is gold and has many silver cat bells upon the vegan leather reins. Her collar is spiked and from the tag that flips toward the viewer, it reads, in Old English script, PICKLES.

The scene:

The land looks like Ramona, spotty boulders in greenish dry brush. The hills have acne. The battleground is right down the mountain from Ramona to San Pasqual, where we played football. They got called hillbillies like we did. Most teams were racialized, other teams were all Samoan or all White or all Black, we were Mexican, Filipino and White. So was San Pasqual.

Dad loved going and walking around the state park where the battle happened. The battle actually happened across the street on private land. The old sign said Mexicans with spears were defeated by US soldiers with the hero Kit Carson who walked all the way from New Mexico.

The tag "¡Seis de diciembre!":

How much like Cinco de mayo! If you go there you'll only hear how the Americans were fighting for freedom and dug up with and reburied honors. Should we honor them? All soldiers? Those involved in a racist holy war of greed? Most history books sanitize the "worse mix of the indolent Catholic and subhuman Indian savage" rhetoric, but it's all there in the primary sources and their acts during this occupation.

The lazy stereotypes about us offended Anglos' notion of who they are, the Protestant work ethic. The Californio lifestyle was a shame, a waste of the land. The argument was that we were subhuman, the worst of two races, so our humanity or right to govern or have property or not suffer didn't matter at all. God had given the land to the White man, no one else knew it yet. Indians were best dead like several presidents declared and later many irregular militia Americans took upon themselves to make them so.

The Villain Flees:

Kit Carson, slips away in the direction to San Diego, a hateful grimace on his sweaty grimy face. Somehow this hero didn't manage to kill anyone in this battle with so many men on his side. At the port city he found that the commander of marines had arrived while the remaining American forces at San Pasqual were under siege.

Background, right:

Mule Hill, the hill upon which the Americans spend the night besieged. A Starbucks and Burger King is pictured photo-realistically on it adding a bit of ersatz and postmodernity flavoring, since as they had no food, Andrés Pico sent the American officers coffee and beef. Ketchup and a coffee ring stain the painting here, devaluing it for some, adding value for others. Stamps of horse silhouettes ring the depiction (Californios did send some wild horses stampeding through the camp to try to get them off the hill).

The background:

To the left on the horizon is the city of San Diego, and from there comes a flying aircraft carrier and GI Joe attack helicopters. Overkill. In effect, what several hundred marines and their cannon were to the small force of Californios with lances and horses.

Background left, the sneak attack:

Californio forces rested at a village close by. Much of the rhetoric spewed and encouraged by politicians and the likes of Carson were that we were subhuman, a first necessity for one group to dehumanize another enough to justify the murder and theft of another group and for them to not suffer psychologically from their acts. Who wants to kick a poor struggling family out of their house on Christmas though they might owe you money? How does one sleep at night afterwards? Call them deadbeats, dismiss their experience and humanity.

The Americans were meant to scout, but the sneak attack failed, they were careless because Kitt had told them they were dealing with cowards. By the time US forces charged, most Californios had gotten to their horses.

Americans charged. The Californios rode off on their horses. It's called a feigned retreat, an ancient tactic White historians often praise Mongols endlessly for where horsemen engage the enemy, retreat, and the enemy front lines charge hoping to finish off the fleeing troops and win the day, only for the horsemen to turn and attack now the smaller, dispersed force who, at a disadvantage, flee into their own ranks, causing confusion, chaos and disorder. The Californio forces were able to stab the hated former provisional governor (appointed when the US took LA and deposed when we took it back). He had even forbade religious services. At some point, Californios almost took a cannon.

The Weapon:

The lance, at first a long cylinder with a wide hilt (gilded) then a shaft of energy that sheds light throughout the scene, becomes loaded with American soldiers cut crotch to chest and bumping into each other in a gruesome shishkabob, the latest one on the end, mouth open in a screech and grips the lance with his hands as they burn to blackened stumps.

Center, bottom:

Miniature American soldiers run into each other, dropping weapons, some fallen into prayer to their deaf god. The American men might have regretted the long trek to New Mexico and then to California. They might have regretted reading *Conquest of Mexico* and imagining themselves as modern Cortéses achieving dominance over us orcs and goblins. They may have regretted how their minds, bodies, and potential were used up by a crusade against the people of an entire continent.

Far Right: Horrible Things in a clause:

The far right is empty of paint. Only the rough weave of canvas shows through.

A spot for the silent testimony of horrible things contained in clauses by those who tell tales like this.

As they rode away from the siege, Californios were jumped by a tribe in the night. Afterwards they, along with some Cahuilla Native allies, attacked the village and killed people in retaliation. It's been called a massacre.

I won't be like US history books and say it was war, it's what happens.

There is context, we need to know it all, and know no one deserves it. The Anglo imagination of themselves is the cowboy, the civilizer, which can't exist without dying Indians, subjugated mexicanos, and Africans. The fight at San Pasqual continues, Chicanos fighting for pride, reminders of their presence, and Americans looking for a sense of superiority and bloody slogans made into actions. It's hard to know what happened. History is often left to jingoistic amateurs recreating the glaze of the cowboy films of their youth.

Because of this, many books have conflicting information. Many books gloss over actions at villages by people like Kit Carson. "While riding back from attacking an Indian village, Carson heard…" In those clauses, if you look, if you can find the testimony or witnesses of the dead, the people there were murdered, raped, erased. Silenced.

46.
Ramona Diary of SRD: A Wetback in China

This must have been the third or fourth night of drinking. Everyone came over to the usual apartment—mine—on Saturday to drink since that was the only thing to do. English teachers and foreign students at a university in southeast China where we'd teach and study for a year. The Austrian students were pissed at me since I had asked them one after the other to say, "Run for the chopper!" and they didn't get it till later. Usually, I was an early ranter and then sat sedately as the speeches got crazier and more demanding and the night got late. UFOs, communism, and American imperialism were everyone else's favorite topics.

All the Europeans seemed to hate America, and complained about it to me, the little yank avatar, not caring I was Chicano, from a marginalized people or that their ass was White. Somehow being from SoCal was worse than being from the Midwest like "the other American." He was also Whiter than me, so there was that too. In my annoyance, I came up with a running joke, saying in Mandarin, "Do you know how many nuclear missiles the US has?" I thought of Southern California and its military bases, technology, and Hollywood, and how it threatened the world with all three. It made me feel like the point man for imperialism, an acculturated coconut from a defeated and occupied people.

I was chill at the get-together. Sitting back on the couch, having a drink. Quite at ease. Glad the Austrians were asking the Other American about the US (though surprisingly respectful to him) and his home state. One of the Austrians asked in their Arny voice, "How do you like Kansas?"

The Other American smiled. “It’s pretty good except for all the wetbacks.”

I jumped up and was in the middle of the room, pissed off, even before I realized I was pissed off.

“What about the wetback in your face!”

“You’re Mexican? But your last name is Duncan!” He didn’t look at me.

“Duncan-Fernandez!” I didn’t expect this shit in China. Didn’t expect my anger at hearing it. “You get one wetback, man, but if I ever hear beaner out of your mouth, it’s on.”

Nonchalant and sedate, one Austrian asked, “Vat is a vetback?”

Fist clenched, crazy-eyed in the middle of the room being looked at by everyone, I explained it’s a derogatory term for Mexicans who cross a river that’s the border.

“Zee udder word, Beanah, is a funny word. Is it because you eat beans?”

All the Europeans were laughing.

“You shouldn’t get angry at funny words like that. I like beans too, am I a beanah?”

I thought about punching the Other American just to be certain I wouldn’t be hearing that shit again. Like always, it would be me against the roomful of Whites who see no problem in their lazy racism and the upholding of its schemas. I felt ridiculous, though still angry. The juxtaposition of the person in the room I should have most in common with, who speaks my native language, is from the same country, created the biggest chasm between us. I sat down, saying, “That goes for all of you,” mostly because they were laughing and telling each other, “You are the bee-nah!”

They went from saying who looked more like a beaner or a wetback to discussing how they were worried about telling Chinese students apart.

My only friends were my pro-American Canadian roommate who believed UFO’s ended communism (not in China) and the Czech woman who sounded like Dracula and had studied literature and missed the old communist days. The Czech chirped, “Vit’s not a vig deal,” and the Canadian told me to, “Sit da heck down and help me finish the beer.” “Thanks.” I sipped my drink.

I looked at the Other American and the Austrians all with ice cold contempt. To them I was the problem and a joke, while it was people like the Other American and the Austrians who had called me subhuman all my life.

I calmed down. Anger isn’t the best response. “Hey!” I called out to the room, “I’ll be back.”

I went upstairs to my place and never went down again.

47.
Ramona Diary of SRD: I Sew So-So

Every summer morning, Grandma would scream, "¡Qué flojas!" The girls would groan, "No Grandma, no," but get up anyway, and one of them would point at me and say, "What about him."

"Never mind him. Get to the kitchen!"

And I'd get to lie there and sleep despite the pots clanking and Grandma's too loud swing music. After a while Grandma would come in and ask, "M'ijo, you hungry?"

"Yes, Grandma." Then I'd get to eat Grandpa's New Mexican blue atole with the dirty looks from my sister and cousins and auntie who was as old as we were. I'd go back to my room and most of the time I got to read the stacks of Grandma's *Enquirers* about furry alien Jesus sightings and how some new saint's stigmata saved an ape boy. "They are true," Grandma told me when I laughed, "You can't trust the TV news."

Later, Grandma would make me sit with her, and she'd tell me things like don't be like your uncle's friend, that White one Andrew and go to school for one thing and then change studies. *Don't switch boats in the middle of the river. A bird in the hand is worth two in the bush.* Her sayings were a relief as my mother would confuse and mix them. At home it was *a bird in the hand is worth two in the river*, but Grandma would tell me how the sayings really went. And then we would sew.

"What should I sew Grandma?"

"Sew something for your conejo." My stuffed rabbit. As I sewed a Sherlock Holmes coat for it, Grandma would tell me I had to learn to sew because modern women are useless.

"They'd let you walk around with holes. They won't even cook for you, m'ijo."

"Modern women" made me think she meant they were electric powered, but I didn't argue.

So I sewed, and by the end of the summer, the bunny had a full wardrobe for every occasion from a 17th century sword fight, to a 20th century boxing ring. Then my friends found out and said sewing was for sissies. I didn't sew anything again.

When I was grown up I'd see my ex's stuffed rabbit named Pudge she'd still keep on her bed. Ancient and foreign, it had been her English mother's too.

Her mother never let me sleep in, even when I worked nights. Small and severe, she chanted, "Wakie-wakie, boy. Time to make your bed." I'd glare at her and say I was still using the bed. While I pretended to sleep I could hear her tell my girlfriend, "Men are babies. They need rules. Train him now, or you'll regret it later."

One morning I found Pudge in the mouth of her sister's dog.

"Your dog chewed my rabbit!"

"Make Mom sew it."

"She doesn't know how!"

"I worked and raised you children, I didn't have time to sew. You're much too old for this thing anyway."

"I'll fix it," I interrupted. The three women looked at me.

"You can sew?"

"I sew so so."

They mostly guffawed but I picked up the stuffing and grabbed the rabbit. He looked like an ax victim. I sewed the rabbit while they cooked dinner, something English. The food was okay, but bland and Pudge looked all right, except for the slobber.

48.
Ramona Diary of SRD: Mi Valedor

The Asshole told me to get his kid a soda, and hurry up. I just looked down at him. The wife of Asshole whispered, "Say it slow, Blaine, he probably is learning English."

"Uno soda, now, amigo!"

They were just in front of me in line. I decided not to pretend to not know why he thought I worked here, so I said, "Screw you."

"Get your jefe, now! I need to speak to him."

I continued to stand, waiting in the same line for the *Ramona Experience,* which from there, looked like Dead Mexican Disneyland. Asshole said, "Are you just going to stand there or should I call ICE." Wife of Asshole said, "They come to OUR country and can't even show respect." Joaquin was jumping in my backpack, meaning chingasos, chingasos, chingasos, but I was tired enough from arguing with Joaquin about coming here in the first place.

I had spent the day trying to sell oranges found on the side of the road to stupid tourists. Problem is, fruit sellers are everywhere and a naranjero with a more honest look took my corner and my customers. Me selling junk reminded me of my mother selling junk at the swap meet during our fall from the middle class. She looked more and more like a crazy bag lady as she loaded up her creaky pickup. And now I felt more and more like a crazy bag man. So the leftover oranges got thrown at parked cars from a bridge. After the last yellow gob exploded on a windshield, I sat down next to Joaquin Murrieta's head. "What the hell am I doing with my life?" I asked him. "I'll never find Ramona's jewels like my grandmother wanted. And who cares anyway? I'm just another broke pocho sellout who doesn't know who he is."

Joaquin, Mr. Gabby Folk Bandit, had been silent for a while, the longest since I had taken his preserved head from his gang, Los Joaquines. He looked darker because now he had the brandy, the goddamn aguardiente, he'd been whining for instead of whiskey that Grandpa Love put him in or the collective swill of whatever I found at the bottom of bottles in the street alongside El Camino Real. Joaquin said, "Everyone feels like that, even your stupid hero Tiburcio said that, and that other guy, saint what's his name. You just need to commune with your ancestors, dude." That was the first time Joaquin had said dude, which made me realize how much I said it. "Where the hell would I go for that, DUDE?"

"Cabrón, I'm looking at such a place right now."

There was an ad on the newspaper I had used as a basket to gather oranges. *Ramona Experience! Meet the Californios! Only 159.95 per head.* We had just enough money for one of our two heads. "We'll have to sneak you in," I told him.

And now I was in line for an ancestral communion. Hipsters also in line looked embarrassed. One's Edwardian mustache had so much wax on it that it looked as if it were made of wax. The Hipster of Wax pushed his sunglasses up when I noticed him and sucked his cheeks in, as if he didn't want to be involved or as if he had passed gas and didn't want anyone to know. My attention turned to El Asshole who yelled in my face, "I am a damn customer, Paco!"

"So am I."

"You don't work here?"

"What do you think?"

El Asshole turned and ignored me. Wife of Asshole said, "Maybe we should apologize, Blaine, he might get violent."

"I'd like to see the spic try."

I let it go. It was more important for me to muffle Joaquin's curses bubbling up in his brandy since our picture had been on the evening news with big letters labeling us "Two-Heads the Killer." People normally don't put two and two together seeing just my head, but once they see Joaquin's alcohol dripping, hundred and fifty-year-old, disembodied noggin, they start adding pretty quick. Also, I came to the commune with my ancestors, not to punch a rude gabacho with short man's disease. Soon the couple, Los Assholes, began arguing whether the pseudo-science of the *Ramona Experience* would counteract junior's Ritalin and forgot me, because what did being rude to me mattered, after all. Even the Hipster of Wax seemed to forget me and be lost in reading the brochure so close that he seemed to be breaking his curly stash.

I paid and felt a little better since Joaquin got in for free and who doesn't like deals or rather steals to be exact. The White teenage clerks dressed in serapes, sombreros, and pasted on droopy 'staches (even the girls had them on like White girls love to do at Halloween, playing un bandido to everyone's "ironic" amusement) this-way-sired me to an old timey confession booth. "Eduardo" explained the various mix of hypnotism, stock footage, "FDA approved" drugs and bullshit that made the cosmic unconsciousness of the *Ramona Experience* possible and strapped me in.

The booth reminded me of the old booths where we would pay a quarter to watch cartoons as kids. Well, it seemed like a cartoon booth and a sex shop peep show booth mixed together. Oversized, colorful grimy buttons. Cameras above the black mirror of the screen where your face looks like a ghost. Mystery stains and handprints. The main difference from either was the disco ball of hypno-lights above my head and the easy listening pop music with the whispery background playing.

The screen read, "Please drink the provided refreshment now to begin your RAMONA experience." Yet, I was hesitant to drink the Kool-Aid as it were—the Ramona Jesus Juice. The bottle with Ramona handclapping above micro script of disclaimers, warnings, and science Latin. I started to pour the Ramona Jesus Juice out in Joaquin's jar, thinking no substance on Earth could hurt or affect him—what has he not lived through, after all? Also, I'm not one for pseudo-science. Then I thought what the hell and drank the rest.

The screen flashed in what looked like satanic patterns and made me convulse a bit. Then a hideous sinking feeling as if all my guts were emptied came on and left me a hollow skin tent. Was I dead? Would I be just another dead Mexican found in a creepy sex booth?

And my head spun and I saw the wooden, low vined porch at Rancho Moreno, the fictionalized ranch of my ancestors, decorated in the Spanish Colonial hell of every *Ramona* movie and book cover. Which is to say a tourist hell of Spanish California meets subservient Mexican beach resort Anglo fantasy. Long story short, it was sunny and sheep were everywhere in sentimental Technicolor.

And El Asshole was there with his family in Hawaiian shirts and flip-flops. He was shouting at white tunic-ed, slick black-haired Brown attendants that he wanted to see some dancing.

Kid of Asshole said, "Daddy, are these Mexicans?"

"No, son, they're better than that. These are ancient Californians!"

I stepped down from the porch. Before I could smack anyone, there was an earthquake, which knocked me down mid-step. A small vibration, then a larger-than-anything-possible-except-meteor-strike quake. Laying on the soft tropical grass, I watched the fantasy sun fall into the lava-filled, ripping earth. I heard laughter as if from the devil himself. La Familia Asshole were all screaming. Then a flood came, drowning us in a bogy, murky liquid the dark color of the aguardiente in Joaquin's Jar. As the brandy-mud flowed down my gullet like that movie where that surfer guy takes a pill and finds out he looks like a mole rat in a septic tank, I had that boring thought that if you die in your dream, do you really die? Then I thought that's stupid, you just wake up and then there was a hand.

Then Joaquin.

The real Joaquin Murrieta.

Or what Joaquin thinks of himself. Or to pursue an even more boring thought, what I think Joaquin Murrieta would think of himself. Velvet, silver, and leather clothes. His face was pale, but I noticed his hands were Brown since it's probably hard for him to remember what parts are White and what parts are Brown, don't I know myself. His voice was like Ricardo Montalbán, Mr. Roarke, your guide to your dreams and desires. (Or Khan, man of vengeance, carrier of your comeuppance.) I hoped he was both.

"Señor Duncan! It is good to see you. Welcome to 1850. How it really was."

Now Rancho Moreno looked more homey than Technicolor. I looked over the landscape of cattle, sheep, wooden sheds, and adobe jacals. A little run down, but not too bad. Kinda like the family ranch in New Mexico.

"Was it really like this, Joaquin?"

"Shit, I'm no liar. Estamos aquí."

We strolled down the dirt road covered with hoof prints and horse dung. Joaquin couldn't resist trying to mess with my head, telling me that this was the real world and I was a time traveler "Like in that movie with that guy with the sexy dumb blond and the purple monkeys," but then he gave up, saying the current California really isn't much different than 1850.

"What happened to El Asshole?"

"Forget him. Come say hello to the rancheros."

Then I met my ancestors. Some of them.

All sitting on a porch, singing and sewing. Women dressed in modest dresses and men in those little coats, Wyatt Earp ties, and side laced pants. All kinda brown skinned, some more, some less.

Joaquin explained to them I was a Californio from the future. The women fretted over me and remarked how handsome I was.

"Future Californios are so tall!"

They were impressed with my love of animals and vegetarianism, making them the first Mexicans in history to say so. They made BBQ tofu just for me. I had to ask Joaquin.

"Where did they get the tofu?"

"They got plates and teapots from China, why not tofu?"

I spoke Spanish perfectly. I rode a horse perfectly with them. I rode at a gallop and pulled a partially buried tofu rooster's head off, which delighted everyone. The old ladies loved me. The young ones told me I was a real man. The men cried and said it was an honor to meet me. They called me mi valedor, my defender, as they called each other. They loaded me with gifts and encouraged me to kill all these illegal aliens, these Anglos, these greedy yanqui traders whose mothers never taught them to only look with their eyes, not with their hands. They gave me a suit of light, a laser gun, and silver crosses for protection against every ailment and every kind of undead. I imagine my own sub consciousness was generating a bit of fantasy for myself.

I had quite a nice time with my ancestors. Yet I wasn't blind to the misery of my other ancestors! Los Indios, whom I saw from a distance, toiled heavily and saw that many were indeed being tortured.

I said something along the lines, "Aren't we Native American as well, why act as cruel as the gringos?" But a lot more eloquent than that. I just can't remember.

The group looked at me in shock.

"Mi valedor, They need to learn to be civilized."

I felt nothing but horror and shame about my Californio ancestors, themselves Indigenous, yet through the horrendous mind fuck of colonization they imagine themselves to be something other than their native cousins. I moaned inside, thinking why must human beings disown each other.

Then the ancient Californios invited me to look, and I changed my mind.

Los Indios were indeed El Asshole turista and the rest of La Familia Asshole bedecked in bad Hollywood Indian costumes. Brown shoe polish faces and black wigs, pale eyes looking at me in misery.

And indeed they needed to learn to be civilized.

The rancheros asked me, as a knowledgeable man from the future, to give their "Indios" a lesson to better tame them. How could I say no? I had manners and expectations to live up to as a guest. Also, I'm not that good of a person. They wanted a Californio experience, so I gave it to them.

Swat! I punched. I whipped. I kicked. I urinated. I didn't quite release all my demons from the cage, though. And I did nothing to the kid, the little neophyte in shoe polish, after smacking him and making him sit still for once in his life and watch his daddy get some learning. "Your father is learning about respect, but you are much smarter than him, right? You know about respect, right." "Yes. No, yes, sir. Yes, sir."

I love kids. Also it's 1850, no one was sparing the rod.

Horrendous things happened to that not-so-nice gentleman. A surprising vein of pent-up anger burst forth in a torrent of aforementioned blows. El Asshole became a stand-in for all the insults, the low expectations, the bad treatment, for all the times I've been treated like an animal by White society, White friends, and White family. Just a fantasy, after all. It's good this guy gets to experience being on the shit end of a fantasy for once.

Joaquin patted my sweat-soaked back and said, still in his Ricardo Montalbán voice, "Ah, Señor Duncan, it's good, show him the way." All the Californios around me applauded as I finished and they handed me my jacket back, now bedecked with silver, along with a new Californio style floppy hat, and my silk scarf from grandma which had lost all its roughness and wear and seemed brand new.

Soon it was dark and El Asshole's lessons were over and the real fiesta began. There I finally learned to not dance like a White boy.

Joaquin came to me and said, "You want to stay here forever? I need some real booze." He was right. The pseudo-science and bullshit were wearing off, faces were fuzzy, and I was gliding rather than walking. Time to leave.

We asked for a confessional booth, impressing everyone with our religiosity. I had impure thoughts from being in the presence of so many beauties, I told them, which caused a round of giggles behind black lacy fans.

Just as I closed the door, I jolted up in the confessional-cartoon booth, back in the real world. I already heard the wailing of the kid and Wife of Asshole shouting, "Blaine! Blaine! Wake up!"

I shoved the jar holding Joaquin back in my leather pack. He was right, meeting my ancestors, learning their ways, even if in my own imagination, my own little fantasy, my momentary bit of pretend, made the world clearer. My own little dream. I may be a broke, confused pocho, but I am no sellout, I know who I am. I am a Californio, and I will have Ramona's jewels. I looked out the curtain to see if the corridor was empty enough for me to run like hell before they started looking for someone suspiciously Brown to blame Blaine's coma on. Just as I darted out with my psychosomatically bowed legs, I heard Joaquin sigh loudly,

"That was some good shit, dude."

49.
Ramona Diary of SRD: Junípero

Junípero, the monk who headed the "spiritual" conquest of California, led the "reduction." He was a destroyer. A strange dude.

Coming upon his statue now (and how many are spread throughout California because he is Saint Junípero now) I expected his eyes to glow and an electric whip to shoot from his arm. He and his brother's army of metal saint monsters would go across the land whipping anyone Brown for having sex. Many of the statues he is paternalistically standing over an Indian.

Rather than some statue, a description of what his day would look like would serve better—recording the death of children and praising it. Keeping men from their wives and women boxed up and crowded in tiny rooms. Damning all the many cultures he encountered as evil. He grew up reading stories of priests in the new world suffering and achieving martyrdom. Like gringos holding onto *The Conquest of Mexico* and pretending to be Cortés as they invaded, he imaged himself as his heroes and came to make everybody suffer for his own glorification. On the way to Mexico City he got a mosquito bite that swelled and he scratched and scratched and became infected and often hurt him. That was not enough pain and misery to generate for himself, he began wearing a sackcloth spiked with bristles and a coat woven with broken wire. He kept a sharp chain in his chamber to whip himself at night for sinful thoughts.

On the theme of repentance he would hoist a large stone in one hand and while clutching a crucifix in the other smash the stone against his chest.

Junípero praised death. He recorded in his annual that joyfully hundreds of Indians went to heaven this year. Our bodies, ourselves didn't matter, only the tally of souls in record keeping.

My ancestor was right there. Many other ancestors were there, Luiseños, Sobobas, and unknown tribes I'm mixed in, those unknown single human beings who don't get names in history. Jose Maria Verdugo, from Sonora, was handpicked for his adherence to Catholicism and was one of the guards on the march to San Diego in the Portolá expedition.

This was his world he took to heart. After all, Verdugo prevented Tongva funeral dances. At least he didn't give the order to shoot all the Tongva warriors (can you call people shoved into cloisters and slavery warriors? People who weren't going to take it anymore, enough to pit themselves against trained men with steel swords, stiff leather jackets, and guns).

If there's any benevolent inheritance of the Californios it's to guard against the Black Legend of using many evils of Spain as a whipping boy to excuse the many, many horrors committed by Anglos and to accept ourselves as Indigenous. The conquistadores of Spain and Mexico via us, their spearpoint in California isn't the Black Legend. California was one of the last colonies and there were limits to its power as many Indians lived outside the system, but it was slavery, cultural destruction, rape, and dominance and theft (the transfer of mission lands to the tribal people was just a robbery by the Californio administrators, Pío Pico here, as happened in other parts of Mexico). I won't defend Junípero. I won't promote fantasies about him. Ultimately, the goal was to make citizens of the Empire by dominance and cultural destruction just as the USA used murder, theft, and eradication.

Junípero still walks California, just as I, but he goes around in stone and metal statues forever passing mission bells erected by worshiping historical groups (swelled with Spanish fantasy overshadowing the horrors, banality of reality). More recent Mexican immigrants fill the rebuilt churches he founded and I've heard some say the monstrosity and torture he fostered was "worth it so they could hear the word of God."

Here we Mexican Californios are praised for our religiosity, the pioneer dream of entering the woods with a bible to bash over the head of simple savages who would all kneel like children ready to learn. Tourist lap this up. And then the horrors, which also get discussed are dislodged from this and the Spanish are villains, the worst of the Europeans. Turistas in flipflops snort Panglossian statements like, "Lucky it's America now," and tell junior to write that down for his school report which will never tell of the California Native genocide the US committed.

My native Californian ancestors came up against an organizational and material world they never imagined existed. They faced alien sickness never seen in California.

Junípero, the self-whipping, cruel separator, destroyer, who praised the death of people he caused by his ignorance, neglect and imperial attitude that his world was better than theirs, can kiss my ass.

I leave with the image of his wounded swollen leg trodding across California spreading its infection with each step as it lands.

50.
Ramona Diary of SRD: Pistola

My sister wanted to know if mom was home. She said:

"You've been in your stupid cave all day, haven't you?"

"I've been reading."

"Come help me get my club fee from Mom."

"Do it yourself, I don't want to be yelled at too." I rolled in bed to face the wall. I read so I didn't have to deal with anyone.

"Please? Otherwise I'll have to ask the coach and everyone will know."

I fiddled with the old paperback. The cover pictured a small group of astronauts pointing to a giant closed eye above.

I only muttered, "Know what," and her nostrils flared. Everyone would know! Everyone would know our family was broke, that we hardly had any food in our big house that'd been on sale for months.

"Sara and Diane are going to pick me up soon, so I need it now."

I let the book slip to the floor cluttered with other fantasy books.

"Is she home then?"

"Let's check her room."

As I got up, I felt as if I were being led to a firing squad, or since it was mom, the screaming, insulting squad, but I always did as my sister said.

We came to mom's door, which was half-open, which it never was. Clara looked at me and pushed the door.

"Kids." Mom fumbled and dropped the gun to the bed. We stayed still.

"God, I didn't know how to unlock the friggin' safety." She grabbed her face. "I thought at least you kids would get insurance. I don't know, then I thought about you without a mother and then you walked in."

Several tears slid down my sister's placid face.

"There's no insurance for suicide, Mom."

The mother and daughter hugged and the mom said, "Sorry, I'm sorry." She looked at me. I didn't say anything. Mom knew that I knew she planned for our entrance.

The noise of honking came from outside and my sister said, "That's for me."

Mom hugged her again and said, "Love you, m'ija." Her first m'ija in a long time. She was back to busted up Spanglish like dad was back to redneck Texan. My sister laughed and said, "I came in because I needed the fee for my club." Mom smirked and said, "Go get my purse. It will be alright."

"You sure, Mom?"

"Yes." Mom wiped her eyes.

She said, "I have to tell them to wait, then. Be right back." She left smiling.

I got the gun. Dad used to take me shooting and once I was older, gave it to me. He called it my "pistola" in that stupid jokey White way of using Spanish. And like many things having to do with dad, it was locked in mom's closet. Forbidden now.

It said Ruger on the side and seemed futuristic, like it would shoot lightning rather than bullets. If mom was dead what would happen to us? Live with dad? Grandma and grandpa? My Aunt Linda, who I always wished was my mother anyway? All those options were so much better than the abusive and manic life we had now. A life our mother expected us to fawn over for as she acted out some kind of play about taking it away where I was… what? Meant to be the audience? Silent. Just there. How many more performances of hers had I already lived through and how many more could be expected? I pushed the metal gumdrop of the safety and set it beside mom who was smiling at the door.

"Here you go, mom."

My mother looked at me in horror. My sister came back in and yelled at me and punched me on the shoulder and back. When I held it, I could feel the pistola, though heavy, didn't have a clip and wasn't loaded.

51.

True Son of Ramonaland: The Real Zorro

So many men have been proposed as the basis for Zorro that one might think his creator Johnston McCulley a dizzy chef, tossing in not only a helping of basil, but housecats and the contents of dust bins in the boiling pot as well. Men such as Joaquin Murrieta, the rebel native Estanislao who marked up burning ranchos with S's, and even the Irishman William Lamport have been claimed. Yet McCully only says he was inspired from Californio history, and who could inspire an aristocrat hero of Los Angeles more than the outlaw aristocrat Salomón Pico, cousin to the last Mexican governor and richest man in California! Here, we find the more pertinent segments of his diary, the fabled party at Abel Stearns house in 1852…

"At the birthday party for George Washington at Sr. Stearns, the wives of the gringos sat silently with ours. Stearns, a foreigner married in, who wasn't for us in the war. 'This is him trying to help us. Now, Salomón,' mi primo, Andrés, told me, 'by introducing us to their rich men, their leaders.' 'He's helping us now that his countrymen, his real countrymen, have robbed us,' I shot back. Andrés told me my crimes weren't so genteel either when I sold 49ers cattle in the day and robbed them at gunpoint at night. I sneered, 'You've seen what's happened to other families of lesser means.'

Andrés used to always talk about George. Wanted to be like him. California can be for the people! Local representation! Federalist ideals straight from the American Revolution. He ignored the other thing Americans were saying—Manifest Destiny. Everyone still asks me why I didn't wear a mask when I was an outlaw. Easy, I shot everyone I robbed. Those ideals were just a mask for George.

My cousins don't let me forget they pulled me from the gallows itself. 'You're lucky that I could smooth things over. We have to do what we can to build friendships with these gringos.'

George. Should I have done nothing? Riding with my compañeros, each of us avenging the wrongs against us the yanquis committed. I wasn't a robber. I'm an aristocrat. I put holes in Americans and from them took out the gold they ripped from our very soil. And who says we weren't keeping ourselves safe? Five yanqui dollars for any dead Indian, and any dead Mexican could be claimed for a reward for the acts of another. I'm sure my rich cousins weren't the only ones to pay for mine.

Los Angeles isn't the town I knew. Maybe what happened, the dice games turned ugly, the gangs roving, the dead bodies every morning is what made me. No more caballeros up and down the street. Only the dank barrio of Sonora Town made up of mexicanos driven from their mines, californio pobres driven from their homes, and indios like ghosts, driven from themselves, telling the vigilance committees, the sheriffs, anyone who'll listen, 'Soy mexicano! No soy indio, I live over there in Sonora town.' They choose Sonora Town because the other natives cast out their village drift homeless on the streets and get pushed in the jails long enough to be bought by a gringo slaver.

That's why they're so quick to don a Mexican mask now. Is it worse than my cousin Pío? I stared at his bushy head covering the whole of the paper he signed at the behest of the American government. He declared 'I am White man!' in broken English to a round of clapping. No Indians or negros can own land or hold office in American law. Our Pico family had the most land so we mattered, so now we are 'hispanos puros' on paper. And it was this, being hispanos puros only on paper, was the problem at the Stearns party. What caused the ruckus with the American pobres. The rednecks. They peered in, hoping for some free whiskey, but were blocked by servants until Sr. Stearns told them, 'No, no rough types. Please leave.'

My laughter floated above the argument. No rough types! I only bought my way out of thievery and murder. These rich Americans make it law.

My laughing got the attention of the rough type and he looked dead at me. 'Miscegenation,' he pointed. 'This is a race mixing party! That won't stand ya hear.' He called out to some others, but a servant closed the door.

'One of your countrymen, Sr. Stearns?' Of course, he didn't meet my gaze. 'I believe, Don Pico, you and I have more in common where it matters.' 'Indeed, señor.' I raised my glass to him but didn't drink. 'And this word miscegenation, what is it?' 'We need not talk about ugly things beneath us.' Stearns apes our manners and he knows I know exactly what the word means. It's been in their papers every day for years. It rides shots of spit that spot my saddle or my trousers from such men outside his front door.

When the rough type man looked at me and said, 'Miscegenation' what did he see? The worst of two races as they wrote in the papers about us, or was I taking after Pío more and more? Would they now have to write the worst of three? I laughed again.

What has Los Angeles become? That party was our last chance to make a difference for our own, Andrés told me. 'Besides, Salomón, do you want them to crowd us all in Sonora Town? You'd really be rubbing elbows with the cholos, then.'

At the party I heard something like the crack of a whip. The front window had a large hole. Outside we heard shouts of, 'Miscegenation!' and 'race-mixers!' The rough type man was back with a crowd of rough types.

Stearns locked the door. 'All of you, get out!' he shouted not outside at the rough types, but inside at us 'hispanos puros', 'Get out, they'll kill us all!' Andrés came running in. '¿Qué pasa Salomón?' 'Unsavory people, I'm sure they'll….' Then my ears rang, a whoosh and a blowback of dust from the courtyard. Andrés, who was at San Pasqual knew what that was. 'They have a cannon! Come with us, we will take our families out the alley in the back…' He yelled after me, but I was already upstairs. I leaned out the top window overlooking the street. No man, especially a maldito like me, travels the streets of Los Angeles unarmed. George. They had a mob of rifles, they had a cannon, against only me, and one, two rough types went down with my pistol. I ducked and then some bullets tore up Sr. Stearns window frame. Then I couldn't shoot back for my own laughing.

That's how the George Washington birthday party at Sr. Stearns' in Los Angeles ended. Our influence also ended since none of the American ricos wanted a cannon shot at their home just for entertaining the likes of us. And we ourselves finally had become less willing to celebrate anything to do with George Washington."

52.
Ramona Diary of SRD: Brown People Celebrating Thanksgiving

When you have a semi-large family, there are many birthdays and graduations. You are supposed to make all of them, and I normally don't. The tracts of desert between Texas and SoCal were my buffer zone. I'm sure no one in my family knew I was in California, and they were shocked I was showing up for something, Thanksgiving even. Yes, it's ironic that we of Native stock would celebrate the American fairy story of welcoming and supplanting that leaves out the betrayal, theft, and blood. But hey, everyone has the day off and the colonial mental screw over is a monster.

I don't tell them what I'm really up to hunting all things Californio. Everyone thinks I'm crazy enough. Personality wise, I take after mom. Everyone else gets along better, is aggressive, drives fast, likes guns, knows more about the world, never gets lost. From what my mother and aunt said, mom is just like my great grandmother Isabel, spoke seven languages but was lost all the time.

There was a long table with a bunch of food. I set Joaquin on the table between the green bean casserole and the non-Southern, hence little butter and no chunks of mashed potatoes. We normally have both Mexican (and a veggie, something for me) and American food.

"Oh, what did you bring Scotty?"

"Oh, I'm just setting something down. I didn't have time to make anything."

We ate. Kids ran and screamed and made jokes.

Everyone saw Joaquin...he was there like he was always there. No one paid him much mind, I saw my cousin chat with him a bit and later some kids ran up and made faces. The kids also played a game tossing bits of tortilla chips in his jar.

Everyone asked me what I was up to lately, the implied silence of where my life is going, this failure or that failure, all that. I tell them what I tell everyone, nothing much! Still, wanting to say something, I told my Aunt Linda that lately I was doing some family research, on the Californio side.

"Oh, that isn't our side."

"What? Grandma and grandpa always said, like always."

"Our great great grandmother was from Mexico."

"Yes, but she was married to Francisco Verdugo. I've seen records!" I had! And the same family names come up, Mercy, Grace, all our names. And everyone living in the same general areas forever, Whittier, East LA, Glendale. Grandma playing at that ranch with that actress what's her name when she was a kid. That nurse from that show. Not Californios? Why would grandma lie?

"Well, what about grandma's dad? The Soboba guy?"

"I don't know. He died."

Are we false Californios? Have I been wasting time? And did it matter if we were Mexicans from California or Mexicans from somewhere else, or the likeliest, Mexicans from a combination of Mexican states and Native Americans from many places.

But what about that old 18th century crucifix, the certificate, the family stories, the Indian rolls, water rights to Glendale or wherever, people arguing, the genealogy I found, the article about my great great grandmother Paula who demanded child support because she had to make baby shoes out of rabbit skin and the papers mocking us, the fallen Spanish Dons, too poor to pay for their children's clothes? The family trips whispered about to Native reservations to visit family and the silence around our Mission Indian heritage. Or the little articles people write when old people in the family die? What has everyone has said my entire life?

"Oh no wait, yeah, I remember now," my aunt said, "We are a part of the California side. We used to visit the reservation. Everyone always said and we got that old marriage license, and all our other family in LA. Ask my cousin if she knows more, m'ijo."

If you are Brown, you know that everyone is your cousin, so I had no idea who she meant. I forgot to ask, maybe because when you are Brown you also get used to confusing things, like a fragmented family history and Brown people celebrating Thanksgiving.

53.

Ramona Diary of SRD: M'ijo Don't Dance With No White Devil

Dad approached mom from across the dance floor of the fandango of my imagination and selected her from her disapproving Hispano relatives. Black Irish Southern charmer with a hint of Comanche, he hid his Southern accent that's unpopular out here on the West Coast, much like we hid our native blood, so unpopular here it was deadly to own up to. Mom with her jet-black hair, flared hawk nose, and redwood skin and beauty. They started to dance. The Hispanos of New Mexico, mom's father's side, have a fable, mostly a warning to girls: Don't dance with the devil. It's an old Spanish tale changed and retold by Chicanos and I'll get to it. It's one Californios lived out and learned too late, one might say, with what happened to our ranches, and our overrun people. Right here it might be good to know about something in Mexican culture called limpieza de sangre. Cleaning the blood, marrying someone more European to "uplift the family." Another thing good to mention is that one of the last things my Californio and Mission Indian grandmother told me was don't marry a White woman. You'd never be happy. Only be with a Mexican. When she told me, it made me mad, not because I was half White, but because both my grandparents tried to keep Spanish fluency from me. Mad like grandma might be if she knew I was telling the world she was Mission Indian, Soboba, something she chose to remain silent on in her old school way. I told her, "Mexican girls think I'm a pocho because I'm bad at Spanish." (Though I do know a bit of Spanish, and I know well the words for sellout as many Mexicans immigrants taunt me in their terror that I am their coconut fate.) Grandma was silent again, but I thought I knew why she tried to keep Spanish from me: survival. Wanting something better, being completely fluent in English and not told you can't do this or that because you're something less, a beaner, a dirty injun, or a spic. As if I didn't get called all those things.

There are many versions of the New Mexican fable about dancing with the devil, (Anaya does his version as well) so here is the gist: A young Hispano girl is known for her beauty. A stranger, mysterious and wealthy, calls upon her at her family's home asking to be listed first upon her dance card. He is moneyed and has been to many places. Her parents forbid her to go to the dance; they tell her the stranger is dangerous. The girl, of course, sneaks out on the night of the dance. Who on la frontera is like this man, after all? At the fandango, she waits and waits. Soon she sees the smiling man from across the room. He thrills and scares her as he approaches. Most versions of the story start here. She doesn't see the sneers of Hispano women or the anger of the Hispano men. The dance hall disapproves, but the couple is captivating. The handsome man whispers the places he'll take the beautiful girl and she laughs and moves closer. Depending on the story, different things happen. The girl might take a breather and be scolded by her mother or be taken by her concerned father away from the outsider, the scoundrel. They argue with the girl and point it out to the stranger. She turns to see what they are pointing at. The stranger, leaving, has a very long demonic tail and his cloven hoofs have left prints seared into the dance floor.

Or, the stranger guides her outside to the shadows, caresses her with his hands and his lies. He is soon gone, never to be seen again and she, in some stories, loses her soul, or later, she gives birth to a little devil with tiny horns.

New Mexicans call little devils like that, like me, Anglo and Hispano, coyotes.

Yet, dancing with the devil is what many Californio families turned to after the US invaded and took over. The laws were in English, the government required greenbacks rather than tallow or hides and there were many murders to steal Californio land. It's not a stretch to see the Anglo as the devil in this story, much less for the genocide, displacement, and enslavement of my more Native ancestors and neighbors in California. It was a confusing, alien and devilish time. It still is. Anglo American men had been coming to California for decades before the war. In fact, their letters home about beautiful, dutiful, but backwards Spanish women and indolent Spanish men who idled the day on song and dance are a big reason we got invaded. The land, they said, was wasted on us.

The land was Californio livelihood and Spanish families hoped an American husband could help keep it from other Americans. Many of the Anglo suitors after the US invasion turned out to be dancing scoundrels. They sold the land and evicted the family.

Mom met dad when he was on leave from Vietnam in LA. Apparently, mom and my aunt were picking up sailors. After that, when Dad visited LA on leave, he'd stay in the old camper my grandpa had that we years later traveled the whole of the West and Southwest in. Grandpa would flash the light on him. Dad asked, "Uh, hi John what are you doing?" "Nothing, making sure you're alone. Good night." Grandpa was a welder and looked like a bodybuilder in the old photos. I mention this to show things were a bit traditional though this was the hippy days of the late 60s and early 70s. I've often been asked if my parents met on a commune and were part of a counter culture race mixing experiment, rather than being part of something common, something colonial, and something very old with precedence.

Back at the imaginary fandango, Dad, slick Gaelic charm making up for his bad dancing a Baptist upbringing brings, jokes and makes mom laugh. Grandma whether being defied at home or sitting there at the fandango clucks her tongue. She always called dad El Gringo. Grandma didn't remember names. She'd shout, hey Gringo, your coffee is ready cabrón! She would tell me to get El Gringo. I knew who El Gringo was, I never thought she meant me.

Dad leads mom away to the dark and I'll leave them there. Later I was born with little horns, a short tail, and an Anglo surname. Grandpa didn't seem to disapprove. I wasn't named after him. Maybe he thought with an English name I would not have to pay the price for being Brown in America. Grandma made sure to tell me never to trust the White devil. At the state parks and historic ruins that used to be our homes she told me this was us and never listened to their lies. In one of those ruins was the place where our Spanish ancestors forbade the funeral dances of our native ancestors. Since Anglos also have their fables of us being oversexed devils in the woods good for nothing but death, like that Billy Idol song, I've always known dancing with myself would be difficult enough.

Californios have been dancing and conceding to survive since 1848 and my Native American ancestors before that in California 1789 and in New Mexico in 1590. And long before that my Aztec ancestors after the fall of Tenochtitlan in 1520. I won't say all these dancers were devils, no one asked so-called settlers to invade, but we aren't all angels. Some of those Aztecs danced along with the Spaniards into New Mexico, and the "raza cósmica" that poured into California danced on native toes. Our Afro-Mexican ancestors still scream their tale through DNA, bills of sale, and ratings of good or bad hair.

In my own cautionary fable, I don't know if mom lost her soul or I lost my chance for one. The conquest is a dance that makes us feel lesser, tells us if we have souls, they're not good for anything. It's better to have feet that burn the ground. This dance that steps into me with the little White devil horns and wild injun partial tail, is the story and the dance of the Americas, of powers at odds, the kind of story you can see in the painting by Orozco of Malinche holding hands with Cortés. This dance of scoundrels without souls and innocents only for a while longer. This dance of few choices.

54.
Ramona Diary of SRD: Sideshow Scotty

I wrapped Joaquin's jar in paper and packing tape despite his screaming at me, "Don't send me in the mail! I won't go through that again." I wondered when he went through the mail, but despite his complaints, he had to be hidden.

I got a gig sitting in a chair inside a cage, I mean a display for my protection like the guy, El Sleazo, told me. He had recognized me in the street as a Californio (as I have all the outward signs recognizable to the learned) and told me he needed a true Californio for his California Exhibition. It made me leery since it sounded like sex work.

All I had to do was sit there as people read a plaque about Californios in the California exhibition. Smile and spin a lasso and now and then spin on the back of my shoes. I said I can't moonwalk, but he seemed confused when I said that. Then he asked if I could do an "Alessandro" as well. I said, "Like Ishi?" but I creeped myself out and he looked at me blank faced. "Who?"

He showed me the chair in the cage I'd sit in, I mean, "Display area with barrier for my protection." This was when I started wrapping up Joaquin, who I kept confused by rocking the backpack he was in and shouting, "Earthquake," now and then. El Sleazo probably thought I was weird.

I put a book in his Joaquin's jar to keep him occupied because who knows how long I will be selling out here, I mean opening myself to other people's interest. I put in my last book other than the *True Son of Ramonaland* which I had transformed into this Ramona Diary, *The Life and Adventures of Joaquin Murrieta*. Joaquin loves reading about himself.

For the first few days I flung myself about in faux soulful ennui posing, watching them watching me ad nauseum and ad boredom. Then the watching was boring as my humanity was ebbing, meaning the privacy to pass gas loudly or to hide the random phrases buried in my psyche that I normally only ejaculate aloud in private. "Kill the blueberries!" Referencing no one and nothing. What's worse were the movie one-liners that jumbled and became some kind of phrasal malapropism or what you call it, a moneygreen: "Run for the lucky punk!" Much more embarrassing than any errant and vocal gas. The first week of tourists staring at me through the bottom parts of their glasses with their mouths half open was rather like having a new girlfriend who wouldn't give you a second alone to yourself and likewise what they (the mouth hanging tourists) considered interesting or cute, hair in my eyes or whatever, I couldn't fathom and the things that caused them to move on to whatever next exhibit I couldn't figure out. The permanent impermanent stare of strangers got normal and my unconscious phrasing got free range. Thus, my cage, I mean display area for my safety, was filled with "Game not my son!" and other jumbled movie one-liners and not gas.

Eventually after the ads, slogans, and catch phrases that society programs oneself with had left my mouth, other things inside started coming out. I started ranting.

I pontificated and thought of that essay hidden in *1984* that I liked so much, the part about a character reading an essay just before Big Brother busts his love nest. No essay in an outlawed book and no beautiful woman next to me, just the lost vibrations in the air of my ideas. It seemed important, like a dream you believe is real that you can't remember when you wake up. Some of the tourists standing outside my cage-display area for my protection began to linger. Oversized forearms banged on the glass and flushed red faces cussed me, all the old stuff from old people, calling me a beaner, wetback, traitor, go back to Mexico.

The commotion caused El Sleazo to come out. I had to keep quiet, no one asked me jack, he said. "Me sitting here is asking. You shouldn't turn me off the minute the answer makes you uncomfortable." "Just keep quiet and twirl the damn lariat!"

That's what made me leave: after all the indignations (I forgot to mention, the pulling up my shirt to show the line of birthmarks, hanging my own mouth open to show my mutant Siamese tooth) being told to be quiet was too much. I left the cage and the tourists who had just been banging on the glass now wouldn't look at me. Some cringed at Kong set free. The cringing and shouts going back to a country that exists under their feet might stop if we weren't tourists and exhibits.

Down the street I tore open the paper around Joaquin, who asked where he got sent. I said nowhere, and then he said, "You have been up to something dark, güero." He also wanted the stamps for his notebook, something I hadn't seen a scrap of, nor would know where he would be able to keep it.

55.
Ramona Diary of SRD: Hey Redneck

My first year of college I hung out with my friend David a lot. He lived in an apartment complex that had a pool, and it was summer in Texas. We were supposed to meet our friend Eduardo who lived in the same complex. It was a large complex, so we were really hoping to see some girls out sunning, but the only ones there were Eduardo and a redneck in an automotive gimme cap and a dirty gray sleeveless shirt. The redneck had a mullet, was paunchy and greasy and seemed old in my eyes, being around thirty instead of a teenager like me. We all sat.

"Hey man, what's up," I said.

"What's up," Eduardo answered.

David shook the redneck's hand.

"Hey dude, I'm David."

"He's not Mexican is he?" The redneck said pointing at me.

"Yeah, I'm half Mexican."

"I don't want to hang out with no wetbacks."

"Well, what can I say? Go to hell, you dirty hillbilly."

David said, "I'm not Mexican, man. I'm Belizean. I don't like Mexicans either."

Eduardo said, "I'm Guatemalan, I'm not Mexican."

"Well, that's okay, but I don't like him being here."

The redneck hadn't moved and pretended I wasn't there.

I'm not perfect. I get angry. I said, "All you gotta do is stand up for me to knock your old ass down."

He glared back at me. He said, "I don't want to fight a whole enchilada."

"I'm the only Mexican here, dude. These two love you so much."

Of course, he would do nothing. It was a hot day for relaxing, my agitating presence or not.

I was more angry at Eduardo and David for not taking my side so they could ingratiate themselves with a random redneck than the random redneck himself. Why they were my friends is a story unto itself, mainly that I didn't have any others. Add the irony that I was half redneck and a native Chicano and not fit to hang out with this greasy, low person who was more okay with these two foreigners. It made me think of college where they called all the well-off foreign students who would leave the states after getting their degree "diversity" while local Black and Chicano students were nary to be seen after the first year.

We sat in the sun a bit, me not talking to anyone. Eduardo had some beer for us, as David and I were underage. It was cheap and nasty but we drank it. The redneck had his own beer.

David asked him, "What kind of beer is that, man?"

"It's German."

"Can I try it?"

He handed it over to David. "Don't give it to him, I don't want to drink after a Mexican."

David reminded everyone, "I'm Belizean, man."

As his lips touched the bottle, I said, "Yeah, drink after that low, dirty hillbilly. Congratulations."

David eyed me, bottle tipped.

Eduardo drank, too.

I thought about asking the redneck questions. There was a good chance of being related to my grandmother's large family of White Texans from Dallas. It would amuse me and horrify him.

Then two other guys showed up. Two guys from Mexico. Big working dudes. The redneck sat there quiet and mad. I talked to them, and we got in the pool. Told me they were mojado, which I didn't understand at first, because, yeah, we were in a pool. "Undocumented, oh, haha."

We played volleyball in the water. David and Eduardo looked at the grim silent redneck and then came into the pool, wanting to play. I said, "Oh, you like Mexicans now?" In the sun, I saw that all our skin color was close, and despite everyone's aspirations to be other things, we were all from Turtle Island. And the silent redneck, sitting by himself on the seat, just turned red and made me feel sorry for him. And, like everyone always tries to tell me, half-breeds are bridges. I would add that we are bridges everyone dislikes for hovering between two sides. No one can ever call me unconciliatory, though.

I said, "Hey redneck, you want to come in and play with us?"

56. Ramona Diary of SRD: Los Joaquines

The head of Joaquin Murrieta and I had been looking, searching, nabbing, and lifting all around California and also ducking away when tourists or strange local Anglos hissed Greaser! Or stuttered H-h-hey amigo in fear. We'd been so busy that I forgot we, or I rather, am a man on the run, and I'm not just talking about every paper showing our faces with the title TWO-HEADS the killer. What or who I forgot were the Head Joaquin's former crew: Los Joaquines, who had to be angry that I took the folk hero's head. Perhaps in the back of my mind I had thought, "Hey Joaquin and I are friends now, he's the big boss, el bandido malo, no problem, right?" I know, wistful thinking, as always.

Anyway, I don't like leaving things behind in what people might call a base or a camp, because it seems that's how you lose things. I'd rather bury it like a pirate. I had buried some of my things and slept on top of it...okay so you might call it a camp. I was heading back up the trail towards it, my head full of the ramifications, locations, and so on of Ramona's treasure, and of the dream I had where the gloriously bathed in blue light Space Chicanos told me not to give up hope and all that. Then treasure and spacemen got pushed out and my night spent with the Amazon Queen Califia wedged in. I tried to mentally clarify these images as much as I could though this was hard since the memories were made when I didn't have my glasses on. The memory of Califia also had been invaded by several remembered half remembered movie posters, so truly her arms, breasts, lips, all those things were quite an amalgam of women, but I do remember her eyes, speckled with gold of course, and her Amazonian grip...you could say

I was distracted when I sat down on the flattish rock by the cactus and brambles where I buried my half a toothbrush and deodorant.

For no reason whatsoever I looked up and saw them—Los Joaquines. Cold urine ran through my veins. Head Joaquin was still in the bag and I worried that if I went to bring him out in some kind of concessionary act I might A. lose his slippery zombie head in an unequal tug of war or B. get shot as they would think I was going for General Moreno's pistola, also in the bag. I only sat there, swallowing nothing in fear despite myself, mouth stretched down like a goblin.

All the Joaquins I had known in my captivity were there, the heroically visaged rocking chair Joaquin, the giant pants stealing Joaquin, the little Joaquin with the camera lanyard, the seven fingered Joaquin, and a few others I did not know. They made a few motions, said a few words. They didn't seem to care that I was there (at my own camp! I mean pirate treasure pit) and seemed to be in several postures of relaxation, laying about here and there. Some looked at daguerreotypes of sweethearts and others played on a had-to-be-stolen and an artifact unto itself Game Boy. Ironically, they were playing a game I knew called *Gold Rush*, and even I thought this was a bit much as the Joaquins themselves were fulfilling bandido roles laid out for Chicanos here since that time.

I then realized why their lack of reaction to my presence ...my clothes, the modern parts were ripped, sewn, and patched and the swiped vintage parts were equally so. What had the Anglos been telling me? "Dang, you look so authentic, is that coloring makeup or tanning bed?" Must have meant that I now looked like a Joaquin. My grimy face twisted in surprise was even on the TV every night like a real bandido. I had a bandido name, as well, TWO-HEADS. I wanted to tell Joaquin right then, "Hey I'm a Joaquin!" But then I kept quiet because I thought I didn't want to be named Two-Heads Joaquin. Moreover, I didn't want to spook the other Joaquins as they might wake up a bit and recognize me as the half-breed nerd who ran off with their leader and a bag of gold dust (hmm, I don't think I mentioned the bag of gold dust I stole before. Why do I always leave things out? I had lost most of it by the time I took it to a pawn shop and showed the man. "Interesting bag. An artifact of the times," he said. "Times?" He looked at me. "The Gold Rush, of course." I looked at the bag close to see if anything stood out. "What's so interesting about it?" "That is some dead guy's ball sack." I dropped it. But I was broke, so in disgust I picked it up with my forefinger, pinky in the air, and asked how much would he give me for an authentic groin coin purse?)

I sat a bit looking at them, the Joaquins. Droopy mustaches added to their depressed look, which only changed as they let out the word orale! absentmindedly or loud saluds! as the bottle was passed around, though these were not as loud as the daaaammmnnn! they shouted as new heights on the Game Boy were reached. I looked at all the guns and knives they had on them, almost like decoration. Were they really that violent, I mean all of them? Could I, myself, even see them clearly? If you don't want to give up who you are, you become some kind of creature to be feared. And no one can really see you, you're just some swarthy nightmare. I thought of me driving around in my old Cadillac. No one could tell it wasn't a low rider. No one could tell my clothes weren't some kind of cholo style, which had to mean thug. I rubbed my dirty pants. I realize no matter how I have been dressed this bandido role has been thrown on me my entire life, and I was tired of it. Perhaps as much as the Joaquins.

One unknown to me Joaquin jerked his head over to me. "Hey Two-Heads Joaquin, are you crying?" I shook my head as I wiped mud off on my face. I wasn't crying for real; I wouldn't do that, I'm not a sissy, but my eyes watered since I expected him to challenge me to some brutish fisticuffs or just shoot me in the face, leaving me with the one head in my sack. Instead he took a bottle out of his vest and handed it to me. I drank. Aguardiente, drink of Californios, of course.

"Don't worry," he said. "We will catch that geeky White boy who stole Joaquin. We have to. What are we without him?"

I drank with them a bit and headed off to pee, but really heading away (get it heading) with Head Joaquin once more. I'd like to say I left my buried treasure of a broken toothbrush and almost used up deodorant with them, but I went back the next day and dug it up. I dry brushed my teeth and then asked Joaquin why he was so quiet for once around the Joaquines and he said, "I thought you liked living, half-breed," and that he didn't care how many sidekicks attended him. Before I left, I saw in the dirt the Joaquins had dropped an authentic Gold Rush ball sack with enough dust in it to keep Head Joaquin in aguardiente for a while and get me a new toothbrush. And maybe even some toothpaste.

57.

Ramona Diary of SRD: A Long Walk With Mom

The crazy lady car that we were embarrassed to be seen in somehow remained where my father's businessman's Cadillac disappeared. The shaking old rusty car broke down when we tried to leave either Alberto's or Del Taco on Ramona's main street at night. Clara had an old red Datsun and was out with friends in some other town. We didn't know how to get a hold of her or when she'd be back since in California at 7 p.m. it is already dark and cold. "Well, can't you ask one of your friends?" Mom angrily gesticulated at the crowd of high schoolers that if knew me would pretend otherwise. "You think anyone here is my friend? They wouldn't if I asked."

"What about if your mother asked?"

"Mom, don't."

I didn't say they'd think we're dirty poor begging Mexicans (which we almost were now though the trappings of our old life still remained, namely the house in the nice neighborhood).

We were in town, but it was likely some of the kids lived in the Country Estates like we did, though we were on our way out with Dad out of a job and moved to Texas. Seven miles to the Estates wasn't all that far, though it was dark and windy and out of the way from town, though in the sticks, pretty much everything that wasn't on main street is out of the way from town.

"Um, excuse me." They ignored her. "No, sorry. It's just that my car broke down and..." The kid in the Ramona High letters jacket and crispy mullet interrupted, "I didn't drive here." She tried several other tables that all continued their conversation and laughter while ignoring her. She came back to the table and I didn't say, "told you so."

"I don't know why they wouldn't listen to me. I'm an adult."

"Can't we call a neighbor?" The neighbors didn't like us that much I knew. Dad had stormed out of the country club when we first moved there and only later answered the question why can't be a part of the country club like everyone else so we can swim at the pool with, "They were rude to yer momma."

Mom said she didn't remember the neighbors' number. She might have been embarrassed, I'm not sure and I'm also not sure who suggested we walk. "We could wait until Clara gets back home." We both knew that could be five hours from now. Mom said loudly perhaps for the kids who didn't listen to her and weren't listening now, that she wasn't fucking waiting around here all night. And it was only seven miles. She kept asking me how far it was as if she didn't drive it every day and as if I walked to town from home instead of just to the little convenience store at the edge of the Estates.

We went the back way to the Estates, the part that goes by Wild Cat Canyon where all the kids race and die. The lights of main street left quickly and the stench of chicken farms and the few trees that followed a creek that made everything colder and feel like stone.

Mom made rude comments just as we stepped along the gravel sidewalk that gradually disappeared. "I don't think you can make it seven miles. Don't expect me to help you, mister. You'll have to carry your own goddamn weight."

"It's just seven miles mom." In wrestling, we ran up the biggest hills and up and down stadiums. Mom sat in an office all day and was middle aged. She always called me mister when she berated me like a June Cleaver from hell.

The sidewalk disappeared. The trees of the creek pushed up right against the road. We had to step over rocks and had only a little bit of shoulder to walk on. Mom was getting tired.

Cars would pass, blinding us like cows at midnight by alien abduction beams. We shut our eyes and looked away so we didn't walk into the road. Every other car would slow down and yell

"Fuck you beaners!"

"Go back to Mexico!"

Or do an "Indian", "HooHooHooHoo!"

The back way was close to the reservation, so mom and I got shit for both Mexicans and Indians, the irony that we were both the local Indian and the colonial affiliated kind, which was not quickly discernable to a passing racist. Or that I had a White father.

"Those your friends?"

"You think those are my friends!" My face got hot and I stared ahead. I wasn't sure they'd stop either. They might say it's dangerous to stop on a dark road like that or someone might see them helping us beaners.

We walked more. Mom gasped again and again.

One car slowed and they threw some stuff at us. It splashed. The dust from cars slowing down and spending up made us cough.

"It's just a coke can." I hoped it was just coke.

We walked more. I worried about getting lost as I do going on even straight lines, but I knew if I found the street that the school bus took a left on and went right, we'd be fine.

More bright lights. "Fuck you spics!"

"Hoohoohoohoohoo!"

"Dirty Indian pieces of…."

I knew that one.

These weren't the people from town everyone called White trash and assumes the worst from. They were in nice cars, more like dad's evaporated businessman's car than Clara's used red Datsun and certainly nothing like mom's bag lady car. The cars made me think of the shiny new truck the guy in *Back To The Future* got at the end of the movie. Spoiled rich kid cars. And their rotten parents.

Bright lights. "Run illegals!" Shut your eyes.

Bright lights. "Fuck you Mexicans!"

Gravel and dust and honking.

A few just spit at us.

Without lights, out in the country, we had just dark, like a black fog, for a while, guessing the direction, my sneaker reaching out to the asphalt road to make sure we didn't wind up on a trail or fall down the ravine. Mom stopped, went on her hands and one knee. "I'm not going to make it."

She belittled me every day, gave me slaps over nothing and always yelled. Called me stupid, acted weird, got called racist names like squaw by everyone and I hated that I was tied to her and that my sister always nonchalantly said we were the same. I couldn't leave her there like I wanted. My family would ask me, "Where did you leave your mother, Scotty?" "I dunno know on the road in the dark with our fancy White neighbors throwing urine jugs at us and calling us beaners." If we stopped, I knew we'd never get there. Only because with a mother like I had, with the town I lived in, I knew no one comes for you. And if they do, it could be Death himself. But really, even if Death is your neighbor he ain't stopping to give some middle aged out of shape Chicana and her son a ride home.

I gripped mom's arm pulling her up.

"I'm tired."

"No one will help us mom, no one will stop." Headlights. Shouts. Clunk. Splash. Dust. I kept her upright and almost dragged her. It was only 7 miles.

We hit the residential area. The shouting distorted moon faces screaming hate at us were less. It was nearly empty in our empty upper middle-class neighborhood. Quiet. Small fires from boys camping out that wanted to work for us anybody with money for them to live or send home. We got home and it was like water on a hot day, like the final collapse from the burden of life. It was like we were home, for one of the last times there. We sat down on the expensive purple floral couches no longer meant for us, but to be seen by those interested in buying the house we could no longer afford. Clara came home 30 minutes later. "Huh, you guys should have just waited."

58.
Ramona Diary of SRD: Going to El Library:

I was tossing a few ideas about around where to look for Ramona's treasure, saying aloud, "Where to look, where to look," and then out of the blue Joaquin said:

"The best place to look is in a book."

"What?"

"El Library, cabrón. Special colecciones."

Gaps in Joaquin's knowledge are amazing, or he pretends not to know things. So, I asked him why he was so learned all of a sudden. And he said being a bandido keeps you well read.

I said, "I thought it made you quick, like you told me when that White guy set all those pitbulls after us."

"No, I said smart. And I didn't get smart reading no penny dreadfuls. When you're a bandido, you look for stories in the news about you. Then you see something else interesting, some new lie they are telling, but then you see some funny cartoon. Then you find a story about one of your friends being lynched saying they were this or they were that, a murderer, a thief, but hey, they were just one guy is all you know. So you clip those articles and after a while you have a little library about things you and your friends do. Then some nerd comes along and wants to write a book about you. Like you and that other half-breed, Johnny Yellow…"

"—Bird. Yeah, I know."

"Anyways, I used to carry all those clippings around with me rolled up and so people thought I had all this stolen money on me. That's why your gringo grandpa cut off my head. But he just got my library, no money, so the joke was on him."

I'm leaving out two things. One, our argument about why Joaquin hasn't been clipping stories about Two-Heads, what the news calls us. And two, his preaching on how little Mexicans like me don't read enough, but Joaquin isn't alone in saying that.

No one ever believes I've read any books since I don't read this or that bestseller and I skipped a couple boring Brit Classics. And then there's the All Brown People Must Be Illiterate reason. How many old, well-meaning White ladies have told me I really should read more because I told them I haven't read *Wuthering Heights* or even *War and Peace*? They don't ask me if I've read Homer or Cervantes, or even Cheever, Coover, or Cisneros. Yet, they are still trying to keep another young Mexican out of a gang by suggesting I read about a bunch of White foreigners learning how to feel or dance toothless in some cottage.

But Joaquin convinced me it was time to go to El Library and I'm also leaving out the very long discussion on which library he actually meant. He kept saying, "The one with Special colecciones!" When we finally got to one where Joaquin sighed out, "Dats it, cabrón," it was a bland modern building with equally bland and modern people pushing in and out its glass doors.

I went up to the Special Colecciones desk and waited. The sign said they had like ten minutes left to be open and I knew that would mean "closed" to my beige ass. When the perturbed looking bald guy came towards me, I couldn't decide which of my White accents to use—the learned and accentless White boy or the Texan. Both can get you out of trouble, but not if you mix them up. I got nervous, so I mixed them up to learn Texan.

"How ya doing, sir. I was hoping to see your Special Colecciones on Spanish Californy."

He did that smile but bare your teeth thing and asked if I saw the sign.

"Naw, but I came really far to see some of those Ramona doo-dads and I'd really appreciate it."

His face changed. Maybe like in *Hitchhiker's Guide to the Galaxy* people really do empathize with being a long way from home, which I was anything but as I'm not only a Californio—I'm El Lay born. Or maybe the dream of Ramona is really magic. The baldy let me in. Even brought the box and tapped on it and said, "Enjoy."

I did. But moreover, what I found there enraged me, and none of it was a clue to Ramona's jewels. I found papers, accounts, an ancestor's passport from New Spain aka El Lay that said he had an aquiline nose (he must be the origin of mom's hawk nose). Also, I found pandering interviews of distant Aunts. And an early Anglo history of the Californios saying we were brutal, savage, yet full of mystique and what I'll call come-hither fuckspictality. Of course that meant it might as well have been a modern history book.

As I sifted through the box, my anger swelled from the weight of seeing how the invader claims everything: not just the land and the effluvia of a family's records, but even the names Moreno, Verdugo—Ramona—for street signs and school mascots. Like they say, I'm a foreigner in my native land. And we the conquered must be assimilated or servile. Become living ruins in the genocide of the quaint.

But my anger wasn't in words just then. It didn't help that Joaquin had started reading *Ramona, a story* and was laughing and I was getting pretty irked having to reach in his jar and turn the page for him. I shouted "Use your tongue, man!" And he just laughed more.

So really mad, I gathered up Joaquin and the box with all the three hundred year old family documents and rushed out. The Special Colecciones attendant's only attempt to stop us was to Hey, Hey! after me, but his reaction alerted the general public which is always ready to do a little policing of Brown folk. In my way stood an indignant retiree in with none-too-real walrus-stash, plaid shirt and fishing hat, a look much like Wilford "Die-ah-beet-iss" Brimley if he had a skinny son. He spread his arms, blocking, but I made to kick him and he held his middle in terror, though my foot only came a yard to his belly. I rolled around him, but then a group of school kids milling about the entrance blocked me.

I was forced to retreat. One kid was pretending to blow his nose at the other children, and any bum rush out would be in his line of fire.

I turned right and saw the teacher—She assumed the same pose of terrified White resistance to Brown master criminals—she spread her arms. I couldn't really fake sock anyone with everything in my hands, so I took the stairs to the next floor. Upstairs, I jumped on a table, pushed up on the ceiling and made it inside. The first few minutes I held my breath, certain they would find me, but then I fell asleep. Then I heard them talking, still trying to find, "That weirdo who stole all that old stuff." For a moment, I thought they meant the walrus-stashed Brimly wannabe, but no, they meant me.

They gave up looking by closing time. When I came down the feeling that I was about to get away scott-free left when the windows I found were too high and the doors were too locked. I couldn't leave without the box, so I lived in the library for a few days (I had no better place to go after all). I slept in the ceiling at night and slinked down in the morning and looked for other ways out with said big box of documents.

The good thing about El Library is that there are lots of places to hide. And hiding is easier when you're Brown, not just because you blend in with the dark of the 70ish ochre décor. I could put up Grandma's handkerchief in a doo rag and become a hood. Take off my jacket and just have my t-shirt and dirty chinos and thumb auto mags and become a low-rider. And, of course, grab a mop and become the janitor.

I read Chicano History in disguise to pass the time and to hopefully come across one more clue to Ramona's jewels. I'd say each disguise was good for one or two books, though I read *Greasers and Gringos* dressed pretty much like myself. I read *Borders Within*, *Thrown Among Strangers*, and *The Culture of Tourism, The Tourism of Culture* like a scholar, but I probably just looked like a dirty nerd with scratched up glasses. The books *Chicano Manifesto*, *Stolen Continents* and *Occupied America* got read in a makeshift hoodie and bandana mask. I soaked in *Insurgent Aztlan* and *Indigenous Quotient* dressed in full bandido regalia. And I dropped my long hair down in my face like a metalhead to read *Conquest, how societies overwhelm others*. I made it through *Foreigners in Their Native Land* and *An Indigenous People's History of the United States* wearing a serape I made from the covering I pulled up from the couch in the back that had native designs. Those were the good books.

The books I read where I thought the author was an asshole I read in the bathroom, as I thought it was fitting. Most of the ones on Joaquin fit that category. He himself was still reading *Ramona*, so he couldn't see I was finding out more about him, or the lies about him. Some of the very worst, the American ones on the Mexican-American war, I mean, damn. Everyone calls the Conquistadors greedy, in it for themselves, killing and thieving so and so's, but what about the US Army and the American settlers? Why do 21st century books still love Manifest Destiny and the atrocities that made our world today? Chicanos appear in US history only when we have something to steal or when they're scared we might take something back.

As I finished reading a page of these Asshole Destiny books I'd rip it out for toilet paper. I really liked the idea, but my butt chafe so much I had to switch back to real toilet paper. And the big industrial toilet roll I found in the janitor's closet gave me the idea of rolling up my ancestor's receipts, daguerreotypes, passports, love letters, and a few good ripped out articles like Joaquin did to his bandido clippings. Sans box I was mobile enough to Judo chop or backhand anyone wanting to stop me. Joaquin had also finished reading *Ramona, a story* and said now that I finally had my own library like a real bandido malo, it was time to go.

I walked out the door, quite happy that Joaquin and I got an education on Chicano History though we had to rip up a lot of books to find it. Yet we had no other clues after all this book tearing to Ramona's inheritance—my inheritance. I almost repeated the words that took us to El Library, "Where to look?" when Joaquin finally said, "Okay, let's get those jewels you've been whining about."

59.
Ramona Diary of SRD: Outside

When I was a teenager and we still lived in the Estates and Dad was in Texas, I never wanted to go home. Home had my screaming bitter mother and my too cool to care sister. I stayed outside, as long and as late as I dared. As it got darker and colder, I watched the sun go down on top of the small mountain across the street. It's supposed to be dangerous in the high desert to be by yourself with cougars, coyotes, cacti, snakes, and you can always fall in the dark. All better than going home.

A few nights, I stayed longer than I dared, where no neighbors could see me from the road. I planned on sleeping on top of rocks. I had my Tijuana shirt and the hood that never fits to keep me warmish. The desert night got louder as the human noises dwindled. All the orange Jello sunlight was gone, and I'd be there in the dark looking at the streetlights below for hours thinking. Thinking no matter what the adults told me or how terrible I knew nature could be, I was safer out here than inside my mother's house.

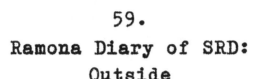

I thought if I could live in Texas with Dad, if I could live with my grandparents or become some kind of emancipated child, and most of all if I could live here, on the rocks outside as the blackest sky and brightest stars came out. And I thought how the ocean, despite my myopia, had shielded me from the creatures of her depths. How the desert always allowed me to step over rattlesnakes, provided a place for me to sit, and protected me from the wind on many nights. And the night itself told me stories with its celestial patterns and lit my path so I never fell. And how my mother had done few of these things. And I felt my real mother was the ocean, the desert, the night. The night that always drew me, the night that I could see all around and feel against my skin, the night which suited my nature and so I stayed outside longer, wondering if they would be looking for me. I didn't even go home from school. I was hungry. Wondered if they would call the cops, none of which I wanted, I wanted to be away from them, a break, a vacation from what my life was. I contemplated becoming feral. Live outside, run away from those who would bring me in and run into the deeper desert and mountains toward the east.

With every hour that passed, I knew it would be worse, and that really, I would have to go in. The Day-Glo watch I always worried about was toxic and said it was 4:26 am. I went in. Silent. Everyone is asleep. Colder inside due to the fans. I went to bed, expecting screams in the morning, which didn't come.

I went to school and then stayed out till 10 pm the next night. Mom in her room watching TV, Clara on the phone. I stayed out a few more times just to be sure. No one noticed, no one cared if I was inside or outside, living or dead, apparently. Even inside, I was outside.

Sitting on those rocks are the core of what I have been outside, watching, or stumbling around gracefully blessed like they say drunks are. And my friends always say I lurk like a monster, an outsider. I hide indoors until it's dark and my kind comes out. I have traveled a long time outside with Joaquin now, even before I picked him up. Do I want back in. Do I want to be back home.

60.
True Son of Ramonaland: Rancho Moreno

Things to Do:

Ground Zero to experience the magic of Ramona! It all happened here.

Be sure to visit the stocks and take a picture of the kids where surly Indians and misbehaving soldiers were bullwhipped.

Background:

Built from the bones of Indians on a traditional grave site, Rancho Moreno has become a park enshrined to the times of Ramona.

Though much of the historical ranch is composed of subdivision, there are markers to point you in the right directions—by the Smith residence's sprinklers is where Alessandro and Ramona were spied upon by Margarita. Under the Whites' kitchen is where the barn was located where Alessandro sang so sweetly to the infirmed Felipe.

Zorro's Note: Peace Tree

Here is where Spanish California surrendered! The valiant General Moreno said, "No más!" In his backward primitive fight against the might of the American machine. Through neglect the Peace Tree has died and its fragments are strewn across its spot by the informative sign. Take a "piece" of history for yourself.

61.
Ramona Diary of SRD: Yo Soy Ramona

You broke in. People related to you once lived here. She lived here. Your family's house. It smells of must. Mold. Now a park for White people in a ritzy White neighborhood where they stare at you. It hasn't been in family hands for a hundred years. Pictures that look like you in the eyes hang around like a grandmother's memory wall. Everything explained by little plaques. A museum to the dead, a museum that's been shut up for years. It's an invader's trophy. A shrine to conquest. Here California surrendered. In the intricate social system of horse borrowing of riding from ranch to ranch (thanks historical markers) two brothers, one defending, one collaborating, meet and decide the fight couldn't be won. What did your relatives think? They wouldn't lose their ranching ways? Tell Americans they were "Spanish" so that they wouldn't get hunted for five dollars a head, though that's what happened anyway with the lynching, the robbing, the raping, and everything else to keep us underclass and the lie that we are the foreign.

Helen wrote the mythic Ramona. Me. The Indian and the White. The Mexican. She wrote us out of history. They say Zorro, Joaquin, missions, ranches, all the past is theirs. They grab the trinkets and wave them saying look what's mine. You raise your voice and they say your people are backwards and brutal. California history is a nice neighborhood park for White people to cluck tongues and feel absolved and great about their accomplishments and ignore the history living and dredging around them. You are tired of other people's dreams. Tired of fighting them. Tired of having to fight them because of what they make you and make of you and make you become.

You sleep in her bed, candles blown out. You think of her—Your past. Your present. Head Joaquin burbles out his own dreams in his whiskey filled jar on the nightstand above which the giant crucifix stands. All the treasures of Ramona you have gathered surround the bed: The Spanish dress, the dog collar, the comb with black hair strands, souvenir altar cloth, all the debris of her legend, but no jewels. Why did you listen to a talking head? Did he ever really talk? Have you just fallen into the left coast national depository of the insane? Who'd notice anyone talking to a corpse here, where no one can see beyond their own falling apart Americano dreams? You get lulled by Joaquin's mutterings till a hand grips yours. A hand like yours, a face like yours. Indian and White. Native-Invader. You fill the basin of the sink with hot water. The hand helps you shave, then pluck. She takes the comb of Ramona and takes the knots out of your hair grown long on the road. She murmurs instructions for you in Spanglish (Como this, that's mas prettier) as the dress slips on, the pleats like iron, the lace Kevlar. Buckskin boots with laces like vines that tighten themselves reach past your knees. Soon you remember everything there is to Ramona, her myth. Because it is your life, it was you the whole time. Your foundation. And you know what you must do.

You chop the old image, the tourist dream, the lazy dream, the misty emblem of the conqueror's conquest. You are Ramona. I am Ramona. Ready for new dreams.

You relight the candles and reach for the giant crucifix above Head Joaquin and his jar. You turn the cross upside down and draw out the box that was always there, that never moved. Your inheritance, inheritance of rings, necklaces, earrings, and broaches. They slip on fingers and toes and necks and wrists and explode in the candlelight. You are a living disco ball, high priestess of California, ready for revolution, what you wanted all along. Joaquin coughs a bubble and blinks awake.

"Qué chingada! Qué chingada?" You allow him to scream and offer no explanation. After the morning songs you both have a task.

62.
Ramona Diary of SRD: The Burial of Joaquin Murrieta

Head Joaquin in my arms. He was out of the jar for this. He cried the entire time.

"I'll tell you who I really am, I'll think of something else to do! Don't do this, don't do this. You dress like a lady all you want, we got lots more places to visit, that's the whole point isn't it, no stopping no stopping ever. You and me, hermanos versus gringos?"

"Joaquin, you must rest. After all this time of swimming in whiskey you have one last job. Don't worry."

"Ah, you are speaking like a crazy person."

"Cycle of life, Joaquin."

"But you'll get your pretty dress dirty."

"You are in an unnatural state, Joaquin. We shouldn't have to be on the run."

I set Head Joaquin right side up so he could see the landscape of rocky hills and dry shrubs empty of people. I commanded the ground to open, but then had to help it out a bit and dig. Head Joaquin still cried tears of pure whiskey. He began humming his own dirge, his old corrido as I put him in.

He kept it up as I pushed dirt on his face and I could still hear the song when he was covered. A small earthquake rippled the hills so my hands fell on top of his grave.

I said, "Joaquin?" and the singing stopped.

Then saplings rose from the ground like hitting fast forward on a VCR. As they grew larger, I could make out green feet, green hands.

Soon complete people were formed and their soft green flesh turned to bark and they soon fell one by one to the ground, steady on feet already. They all looked like Joaquin, some dark, some light. Short hair and long hair. They formed lines, battalions that filled the empty hills, and began singing a new song. A song about Ramona. A song about me.

63.
True Son of Ramonaland: Relevance of Ramona

It's true that the land is sick, that many Americans don't believe they need Ramona, even *IN* Ramona. They think she is merely an old tale like Paul Bunyon: just an element of local color. They rush through our state, tread upon our cultural treasures, and head for the beach to soak up sun and spot dolphins. They may not even be too concerned that they are in our state and recognize only that they relax upon the edge of the platter of the USA. Too many vacationers blunder through California blind of its history and people and the giant figures that lead them. Such 'quaint' ideas die in the melting pot subdivision mentality. With each turn of the page of this guidebook, Ramona lives again, the land has a queen.

Only efforts like this book are a bulwark against the cookie cutter society, the evenly baked citizen clone that can only remember its personal history, allowing the rich world to be hidden from him as it does not compute with his programming. Dear reader, if your GPS broke and the gas station lacked all maps save this manual for Ramona California, your first and only foray into the past, Lord help you. I, Zorro, would curse such a life if it were a life worth living. Our hope lies in the tiny, too indulged hands that turn these scoffed at pages, and in tiny eyes that peer with knowledge at sights that you wiz by. Dear child of ignorant clods, dearest last chance for a new America, I welcome you to California.

64.
True Son of Ramonaland: Back Home

Now it's time to put it all together! Before the last bag is unpacked and the mundane workaday takes over from the timeless mind of the vacationer. Did you see Mission ruins or Ramona's and Alessandro's Cabin? The San Andreas Fault? The Peace Tree or *Roble de Paz* as said in Spanish? Do you appreciate the Indian and his woes? Has your life been enriched by the Spanish lifestyle you have encountered? Do you now feel even more American? And how was the beach? Will what you saw fuel your way through the burdensome modern world enough till your next visit to the land of dreams. Use the space provided before the return to life rubs away the details of all the wonders found from your Grand Tour—nay your American Pilgrimage. Perhaps now is a good time to press in and label the flora you found as well as the dimensions of the Indian footprint you plastered or the sketch of the stack of *Californio* skulls you viewed or, moreover, the head measurements of any live ones you were lucky enough to enjoy the hospitality of.

Again, if you got this book secondhand and some less enlightened traveler has filled the space with their blather, use the margins! By now you've learned how to make do. California's wonders call for every hand to depict them.

65.
Ramona Diary of SRD: Home Again

Zorro's guidebook needs to go. I've written over it and pretended all the pages were blank, but when you write over text you can't really read what's new or see what's underneath. And this is the last entry: I'm afraid this bundle of papers might explode if I add anymore, and I'm tired and want to sleep. Whenever and wherever I wake, *The True Son of Ramonaland* and the world it imagines will still be there. But I'm putting down what happened, and what happens now. My own dream.

I am Ramona. The Green Joaquins are my brothers. They grow in my garden with the face of Joaquin the Defender of California. I am Ramona. Hence, Zorro, a California tourist, hobbyist, culture-vulture, settler—Ramona lover—came looking for me.

His real name was Neil. And I knew what was in his head. His mind. Zorro was no longer the corpulent and sedentary collector—he was now a slim adventurer—in fact I'm sure he imagined himself a 20st century dime novel hero as he broke into tombs and stripped family heirlooms from skeletal necks in the name of science and anthropology and a complete collection. Better with him, he thought, than the dead or some ignorant and simple descendant like myself.

Neil probably felt damn lucky to have the name "Zorro" in the public domain and be allowed to use it and live his fantasy legally. He signed his name everywhere Zorro! And people gave a little laugh. For real? For real, querida! I am Zorro! And now who could stop him? It was Fall, sheep shearing time, the same time of year *Ramona, a story* had started. Inspiration had led him to the beginning, Rancho Moreno, a place he had not been to in years. This is where the Peace Tree was, after all, where Mexican California surrendered and where

Ramona must surrender her last mysteries to him. Inspiration, clues, and this had to be the place that scoundrel, SRD had wound up. Using his real name, how utterly lame and unimaginative. Zorro needs no other appellation.

Yet this was the last place the jewels should be—the book, the only book, tells us that they were left in Los Angeles in a safe place. Or spread everywhere like those cheeseball guide books say. There, or, Zorro would probably shudder at the thought, *MEXICO*.

I pushed Zorro's mind aside. My journey and search had brought me here. I'm only guessing at his inspiration. Why was he here?

He passed through foliage, past the Peace Tree, and came down the sandy path. His own senseless living-in-the-past path of life must have made sense now as it all walked up to this moment, this vision of beauty, me sitting on the bench at my ancestor's ranch, a bucolic-exotic garden. Zorro fell to his knees, the vision of the Sweet Lady had chosen him, as he suspected all along! The dumb tourist legends were true! He knew he would be King of California. His dream of Spanish California must have been fulfilled. He took my hand. I peered at him over my lacy fan. His face had the ecstatic beatitude of a Rococo ascension.

"Ramona! My lady, I have sought you through deserts, through mountains, nay through centuries! Through…" I removed my fan covering my beard. "Hello, Neil." Zorro quivered.

"May I have my hand back?"

His eyes passed over my dress, my long brown hair, and despite himself, my hairy chest. Then he saw the pearls, the rings, the damask, the silk, the stone bespeckled fan. He saw them all: The Jewels of Ramona. My jewels.

"You thieving Beaner! Those are mine!"

I made no response. The foliage, the flowers, the fruit-trees shifted. What Zorro had thought were bushes and trees at once pressed him so close he could see that they had faces, faces he knew too well, as once he was forced to kiss the original—Joaquin Murrieta's. Green Joaquins held him still in their vines and thorny branches.

I had his belongings stripped, though I let him keep his silly hat and mask. He wailed and burbled a bunch of why's. He still wasn't used to the way things are in California, despite all his talk and life goals to steal everything Californio. But his things on the ground told me the story.

Zorro was at Rancho Moreno because had been following me. He made me his unwilling personal cicerone as Joaquin was mine. He had fake beards and several tourist Hawaiian shirts and shorts, tall striped socks, sandals, and ill-fitting polo shirts. He was the walrus-stashed retiree at El Library. The hooded man at the Ramona Wishing Well. That Cinco de bolo guy at the fandango. He also had a digital camera. Photos of his trip, photos of Joaquin, photos of me. He was the one who stole Joaquin at the Ramona display at the California museum. Joaquin had mentioned when I finally found him oddly placed on a bench that he had to bite that White guy again, but I had no idea what he meant. I just took it as another manifestation of his fragmented memory and assumed he had to bite a lot of White guys like every Chicano. I didn't think he meant Zorro necessarily.

"Really man? You pulled that *Lolita* villain stuff?"

Zorro said nothing on the matter, though he looked a bit cowed like my dog Buster when he just farted.

In Zorro's pack, I also saw that he had Ramona antiques I missed or couldn't find. Señora Moreno's prayer beads. Felipe's razor. He also had a list from "Grandpa Love." Zorro was my maybe cousin.

The Zorro junk told me all about his trip, mainly that Zorro hijacked mine. Only one thing was missing from his pack.

"Where's your Ramona diary?"

"What diary?"

"You only took pictures?" But then I realized what the diary was for. Conquest sealer. Like with Vercingetorix in chains, but instead of being dragged to Rome, it's as if Romans went to France to see him in defeat. To see the beaten "savages" to sleep better at night. I gravitated towards my own diary because I'm a reclaimer.

I also realized what tourist photos were for and why Zorro would choose them over a diary. A refrigerator. The land is the past and the tourist is the modern. The ruins are the ruins of the other. Words can offer overt meanings. Tourist photos like the Ramona novel, like the invasion, like the Anglo imagination freeze the past in the Southwest. He, the tourist, is the actor, the poser. We, the Native, are the backdrop in his quest for the frozen and the ever-dying quaint.

I was lucky the Joaquins broke my camera back at the bandit lair.

Boring slide shows have no real context, no meditation. My own diary turned the tour inside out—I am Ramona touring herself, kicking out the tourist infestation. Background coming to the fore.

I erased all the photos on his camera. I could feel time slip forward a bit. A few power lines went up, the houses around got more modern, and Rancho Moreno itself had solar panels.

Zorro twisted in the hold of the Joaquins' branches.

"Those are my private records of my anthropological expedition, how dare you! You backwards ignoramus. You hate science! You hate education!"

"Science? For real?" Green Joaquins and I laughed.

While looking around for someone to stop me destroying his "scientific" photo album, he noticed that below the drying chili peppers were shelves made of racks of skulls pierced with long poles stacked on top of another.

I noticed him looking and said, "They're called tzompantli. I'm bringing them back. Quaint right?"

"Those have nothing to do with Californios. Just Meso-American barbarism."

I laughed. "They have a lot to do with it now, Neil. You'll see things differently when your head is there."

Zorro, though now a brave adventurer, watered his pants. "Please, not my head."

I patted his back. "Think of what you'll be. Good fertilizer for Joaquins. Try to be a superfan of the future instead of the past."

I told Joaquins to take him to where Felipe, brother of Ramona, convalesce with the help of Alessandro's singing. The room, which of course was now the basement of a family aptly named White. They were on vacation and missing out on the renewal going on here.

The room was now a musty cinder block storage area, not a quaint barn where Felipe languished.

Even when tied to a post and given the Whites' dog's bowl of kibble and water, Zorro cursed me. I had the Joaquins move the tzompantli down with him. A human head did me good after all, maybe a dozen would help him.

The Anglos here still saw the Moreno Ranch as a public park. Maybe they thought me and my Green Joaquins were from a kids show. When Zorro screamed and pissed himself, the lady with two toy dogs and the too fit jogger in a future onesie didn't even stop. Being your real self will do that. Most people don't want to get involved.

I had matters to attend other than Zorro and people picking up their dog shit.

It was revolution time at the Moreno Ranch. The griffin egg Califia gave me had hatched. I named the griffin kitten Pickles after my childhood cat. I was also busy making up my mind. Reforming Rancho Moreno to suit me and my dream. I organized Joaquins and considered the building of a colossus of Ramona and a beacon in her eyes to call all the Space Chicanos home or have the rocket ship hiding in Vasquez Rocks lauch. While I thought about these and other things, in the basement of the Whites, Zorro and his costume got even more raggedy, his beard scruffier. His Zorro mask fell off. Now he had the look of a pioneer. Mountain main. Bear Flagger. Ranger.

Like I said, I was feeling sorry for him. And I had the Joaquins let him go. After all, he was my maybe cousin. He ran straight out, pantless. Wordless.

I made some decisions. The Moreno Ranch was Ramona's, finally. Mine. I raised my griffin flag. The Griffin Republic of California.

I wasn't breaking too many laws, but the police kept their distance as they do when confronted with an army of animated revolutionary plants led by an angry Chicano cross-dresser. Joaquins stood impassive, swayed in the wind, and never raised their voice. We even welcomed guests. For a little while until they became bad guests.

Meanwhile, I smashed the Spanish California fakes and put all the Ramona relics to use, the signal bell, the hoes, the lariats, and had Joaquins build modern Californio artifacts: The holy laptop. The magic phone. Green Joaquin supercomputer AI.

And while more Joaquins grew, the policía politely asked me what I was doing. I felt no compunction to answer, and, then, Zorro came back.

After overcoming his fear of my tzompantli and finding new pants, Zorro felt it was his duty to warn the world. He thought he knew us since he was an aficionado for cuisine and baskets, and, thus, hip to what was going down. Yet he found the world he knew already was changing before his eyes. Indeed, Joaquins were setting up signs in Spanglish around the Ranch and he saw the replica relics of the past he had come to love smashed.

And so there was a rush to mob us and Zorro was at the fore. The Anglo tradition of the lynch mob, the socially sanctioned yet extralegal band gathered about the gates. They saw themselves as the good people of America. Zookeepers of the Southwest.

All the varied rednecks of California were there—the desert necks, the mountain necks, the valley necks, the surf necks, all those who want to keep us down and enforce a racist society. Just like the Bear Flag Republic pirates. As much as I wanted to change everything, it was old times rearing their ugly heads everywhere.

Zorro's response was predictable. He had to flip from the noble child savage image of his imaginary friends, the old timey forlorn nostalgic play land of his lost childhood to the dirty savage of the threat to the White race. You can do anything to a savage, and he was here to civilize us with his friends and guns. How dare anyone interrupt his fantasy.

The police didn't do a good job policing the people brandishing weapons and shouting for the death of others. These were the good citizens acting within their rights to lynch. Much worse were the "allies."

At first, I waved at the joggers, the doggers, even put up with the shouters—what could anyone do? And what was I doing? I was finally me. I was home. They showed up with "Ramona!" and "Pickles lives!" signs. They seemed like good signs to me and I let the hippies in. Soon enough, they were liberating everything, from the house, from Joaquins, and telling me what soil I should use, and demanding to know what WE were doing next, and then telling me what it was. They even tried to correct my Spanglish. When I made decisions, they said, "Whoa, whoa shouldn't WE vote on it?" I told them this is my house. "Yeah, but WE are here, this isn't just about one bean-I mean just you." I kind of lost my temper and spanked some of them—well, I organized Joaquins into spanking brigades before I let the hippies out. They cried and asked, "what did they do?" I told them to go home and have a think. Californio hospitality has its limits.

During all this Brenda Linda Something showed up and gave interviews, as they weren't airing her exclusive about her "Sex Encounter with the Two-Headed Killer" anymore. "I know it's the killer Two-Heads. I'm like, so in his spell. I know he wants to kill me, but I still want to go in there and hold him." She smacked her gum. "He's hypnotic." Seeing Brenda Linda Something's interview made me miss Califia, but I didn't have much hope of seeing her again.

On TV, reporters were still insinuating about my, about Ramona's, lack of credibility. The news sent all their token ethnic reporters to the ranch. The Tokens stood around with pursed lips asking questions and inching closer to the gates of Rancho Moreno. Having gotten bored of airing all the Rangers' racist remarks and calling them "controversial" they asked to talk to me. This was only after trying to get an interview out of several of the Joaquins, who, as I said, were in no mood for talking after being a head they never listened to for a hundred and fifty years.

The news lady insisted on calling me Mr. Duncan and not Ramona, so I showed her the skull racks. She called me Mr. Ramona then. I gave her a little Joaquin tea (don't ask what part of a Joaquin the leaves come from) and she calmed down enough to start the questions.

First thing she asked about was, oddly, the dress. I said, who cares, it's pretty.

"What do you want to talk about here, then?"

"How about respect? See what I had to do just to get you to call me by my name?"

She ignored that. "What's all this....controversy about?"

"This battle is for my personhood and history."

"Anything else."

"If I think of anything else, I'll let you know."

"What about all the violence?"

"What violence? What the heck are you talking about?"

"And what is that on your shoulder?"

"Oh, it's a griffin kitten. A gift from someone named Califia."

Then she asked the last question, which I thought should have come first.

"Are you the real Ramona?"

I had wanted to say this is The New Chicano Hope, Old California Strikes Back, The Return of the Californio, but even I was tired of malapropisms and call backs. "Real or unreal, I'm here."

The Rangers tried to push in. But what could they do to Joaquin? They cut his head off a hundred and fifty years ago, and yet he is still here. What they cut grew back in a matter of seconds. The massed police did nothing to stop their violence. We, the Joaquins, the Ramonas, were the evildoers for refusing to stay invisible.

Looking at their contorted faces hacking and pushing into Green Joaquin nettles and branches and immovable trunks, my dream almost got ugly. Space Chicanos burning all the tourists or a mass exile came to mind while I pondered what's the use of being who you are when you get pissed off all the time at the hate-filled world. Yet, my Ramona trip taught me to dream better than to become an asshole myself. In other words, I had an idea.

After the Rangers had run back, amidst all the general shouting (from their side, Joaquins were ever silent) Zorro called me out. I knew he had an idea of his own and I knew it would involve me swinging from a tree.

He shouted, "Hey Scotty!"

"Ramona."

"Whatever, ya ready to give up?"

Zorro jumped on someone's car for drama.

"One fight. You and me for everything. If I win, you give back everything you took."

Of course, that made me mad. His boots dented that guy's car for no reason.

"What are you scared of, beaner?"

"Ok, it's your funeral."

I still had my idea. I agreed to step out of Rancho Moreno. The Rangers agreed to move back a hundred yards, except for Zorro.

Joaquins combed my hair, brushed down my dress, and wiped my jewels till they sparkled. I looked nice. If bandidos need style, Ramona needs grace.

And I stepped out the gates of Rancho Moreno.

I looked into the Ranger mob of faces and saw everyone. Saw kids from school, cops, condescending teachers, newscasters, LA Migra, my White uncles who taught me wetback, wannabe militia that might as well be KKK, Anti-Chicano Voting Retirees, small town hoods who beat migrant workers, those that do worse, frightened nopal en frente sellouts, angry Anglo Ranchers who forget how they got their ranch—in other words Grandpa Love and his Rangers. All the people I have ever known who hate unthinking, imaging themselves righteous, all unified and screaming. The Americans who hate us, los Californios, los Chicanos, los Indios.

The sun was out, but I still needed more time for my idea.

The mob of Rangers pushed Zorro forward until he stood in front of the forest bandidos of Green Joaquin Murrietas.

Zorro looked like me before I became Ramona, ragged, floppy hat, 19th century clothes. Except now he wore an unofficial star that made him some kind of policeman. The official unofficial law.

"Where is your whole enchilada now? You ever fight mano a mano? A fair fight."

His voice echoed some stupid John Wayne bravado. I knew he was scared. I also knew the fair fight he wanted—a fair lynching.

He said, "I'm gonna mess up your pretty dress."

"Then what are you waiting for, Neil? You seem to have forgotten about last time after all."

Zorro stood ready, twitching, humming.

"What the hell are you humming?"

"None of yer business."

"Can we do this without a sound track?"

"I can hum if I like."

It was a theme from an old cop show. *Barney Miller? Fish? Law and Order?* Very distracting.

Zorro charged me, screeching, untrained wide cowboy punch already swinging. And I gut-kicked him in reaction. Unintentionally. Knocked the wind and knocked him out. Flat.

I needed more time. I picked him up, feigning a struggle. I fell back and held him on top of me. I shouted, "What's that, Zorro? America will never give up to some dirty foreign spics like myself?" Variegated rednecks hooted and hollered at that. "Get 'em, brah!"

Blacked out Zorro's mouth emitted a line of drool that hit my face.

I yelped, "No! Gringo might is so powerful!"

"HOOOO YEAH! Rip dat Beaner a new one!"

I let out "We must succumb to the power of the real Americans, oh no, oh my," but then I realized, I heard nothing, no hillbilly hooting or bleating. I pushed Zorro off me.

Zorro woke up face down, sputtered dirt. "Now! Get him now!"

The rush the Rangers had planned—the official unofficial lynching—wasn't going to happen. I didn't need that long, just a distraction, like TV, or two maybe cousin nerds fighting.

My Green Joaquins had grown in the field of Ramona around all the Rangers and had their thorny arms around them. The show had kept them from noticing that around them, between them, and through them vines of Joaquins had been growing, wrapping. When they noticed, it was too late. Joaquins had encased them like bark.

"Your violent fantasy isn't going to happen."

Between air gasps, Zorro said, "But you are a killer…huh… a savage. Huh! What about your ….huh…skull racks, the zha….. huh…zhua…huh..a chomp…huh…."

"Tzompantli, and they're replicas. Décor. Clay."

All the Rangers were trapped—cowed—inside the Joaquins. No more dead Roble de Paz, but living Joaquin Caretakers. It would hold the Hate Rangers still until they were better people. Until Joaquin grew in them and they couldn't tell the difference between Bandido and Rangers anymore. Symbiotes. Finally a part of this hemisphere, Turtle Island, Cemanahuac, call it what you may.

They had Joaquins. Like I had. Joaquins interested in clean air, clean land as they were half plant and dependent on them for life. They would have that Californio hospitality of welcoming to strangers that Helen Hunt Jackson enjoyed and scribbled about. And if any of them wanted to do something foolish, their Joaquin would prick them hard with a spine or root them in one spot and grow thorns into them until they learned better.

Yet there would be no Joaquin tutor for Zorro. No Indian guide, no cicerone, to slap his grasping hands, to open his eyes to what could be his own home. He was a hard case.

I picked him up and placed him in the Whites' basement. I put up some mirrors so he could find out who he was and stop being other people.

And how could he stand to look at himself sans costume? A Hate Ranger. Part of a culture that makes a racist like Zorro the norm, how could he like what he saw? Maybe my kick reattached some ocular nerve so he could see outside the Anglo planet that told him they were the only ones who matter, the ones who belong. What he saw only made him scream. He screamed so much he shook the house and scared my griffin kitten Pickles. We shut the door. Some people.

And maybe the door is what did it. It completed some equation and via the acoustics, location, and fissure alignment of Felipe's room, which is the heart of California and its conflict. Both the surrender place where natives and invaders meet and the singing place where connections are born. A place that must connect to the San Andreas fault. I surmise all that because Zorro's screams shook not just the house, but the land. Like the way Joaquin said the Devil did. El grande. The big one. Zorro the crying devil.

As houses fell and their banging mixed in with Zorro's screams, I grasped for my griffin kitten Pickles who flew off, and I accidentally stepped in dog poop. I hopped with one leg out, looking for a clean area to wipe my fancy shoe on, and so I was distracted from the shaking quake, the screams of Zorro, the screams of everyone, and the falling, crashing houses.

When my shoe was clean, the shaking stopped, and I saw Joaquin leaves and twigs everywhere. TV crews, la policía, Brenda Linda Something, everyone gone but me and the Joaquins and their charges amidst the debris and Rancho Moreno, which was built by my own great great grandfather and has stood these many years.

And the coastal breeze from the east made Joaquins' branches sway in new ways, and so I knew. We were an island again, for the first time. The isle of California. Ramonaland.

Then I noticed Rancho Moreno changed color, becoming shiny. My dress, my skin, my bones all became gold. In a light as golden and blinding as the light reflecting off Bunny Wigglesworth's ultimate Zorro outfit at sunset. I heard her voice, felt her strong grip. I turned and saw beautiful Califia and her Amazons from Aztlandorado. She lifted me in her grip and kissed me. She then walked inside Rancho Ramona and sat on the only chair left, making herself right at home. (Were we together now? Did it matter?) My griffin-kitten fluttered above the golden Amazons and green encased Ranger-Bandidos.

Dreams meet in California. The dream of Rodriguez de Montalvo and Hunt Jackson. The older dreams still dreamt of the Luiseño, the Chumash, the Kumeyaay, the indocumentados from the Mexico that is cut off by only imagination, and even the dreams of those invaders, the tourists, the forty-niners, American whiners who know in their deep-fried hearts, their dreams are shaky as the land. For me there is California—the island nation of Los Californios, no matter its origin, the notion I upend and take back. My dream I live so I can go into the world, the other California that may always treat me like a tourist instead of Ramona.

About the Author

Scott Russell Duncan, a Xicano writer, was editor on the first Chicano sci-fi anthology, *El Porvenir*, ¡Ya!, which was a finalist in the Next Generation Indie Book Awards. He is director of Palabras del Pueblo, a writing workshop for la raza. In 2016 his story "How My Hide Got Color" won San Francisco Litquake's Short Story Contest. His nonfiction piece "Mexican American Psycho is in Your Dreams" won first place in the 2019 Solstice Literary Magazine Annual Literary Contest. He is at work on a collection of short stories called *Plurality*. His novel, *Old California Strikes Back*, a mix of the reality of growing up mixed-raced and of a fantasy tour of California with the head of Joaquin Murrieta was published in 2024 through FlowerSong Press. www.scottrussellduncan.com

Previously Published Material

"M'ijo Don't Dance With No White Devil"
Pithead Chapel Fall, 2017

"The Head Joaquin"
Label Me Latina/o, Fall 2017

"My Heart is Bathed in Chilis"

Somos en escrito, 2016

"The Car"
Dogwood Literary Journal, 2016

"Mi Valedor"
Somos en escrito, 2015

"Wrath of Mom"
Diagram 2015

"Captain Kirk Isn't A Doll Like That"
Label Me Latina/o Fall 2013

"Fernando's Testimonial"
Border Senses Summer 2012

Printed in the USA
CPSIA information can be obtained
at www.ICGtesting.com
LVHW091116211024
794380LV00003B/12